THE
FACTS OF
LIFE

And Other Lessons
My Father Taught Me

LISA WHELCHEL

Multnomah®Publishers *Sisters, Oregon*

THE FACTS OF LIFE AND OTHER LESSONS
MY FATHER TAUGHT ME
published by Multnomah Publishers, Inc.
© 2001 by Lisa Whelchel

International Standard Book Number: 1-57673-858-2

Cover image by Tony Stone Images

Excerpt on pp. 141–3 taken from *Creative Correction,* by Lisa Whelchel,
a Focus on the Family book published by Tyndale Publishers.
Copyright © 2000, Lisa Whelchel. All rights reserved.
International copyright secured. Used by permission.

Scripture quotations are from:
The Holy Bible, New Living Translation © 1996. Used by permission of
Tyndale House Publishers, Inc. All rights reserved.

The Holy Bible, New International Version (NIV) © 1973, 1984 by International
Bible Society, used by permission of Zondervan Publishing House

The Living Bible (TLB) © 1971. Used by permission of Tyndale House
Publishers, Inc. All rights reserved.

The Holy Bible, King James Version (KJV)

Contemporary English Version (CEV) © 1995 by American Bible Society

The Holy Bible, New King James Version (NKJV) © 1984 by Thomas Nelson, Inc.

New American Standard Bible® (NASB) © 1960, 1977, 1995 by
the Lockman Foundation. Used by permission.

The Holy Bible, New Century Version (NCV) © 1987, 1988, 1991 by
Word Publishing. Used by permission.

Multnomah is a trademark of Multnomah Publishers, Inc.,
and is registered in the U.S. Patent and Trademark Office.
The colophon is a trademark of Multnomah Publishers, Inc.

Printed in the United States of America

For information:
MULTNOMAH PUBLISHERS, INC.•POST OFFICE BOX 1720 •SISTERS, OREGON 97759

Library of Congress Cataloging–in–Publication Data
Whelchel, Lisa.   The facts of life and other lessons my Father taught me / by Lisa Whelchel.   p.cm.
ISBN 1-57673-858-2 (pbk.)   1. Whelchel, Lisa.   2. Christian biography–United States.
3. Television actors and actresses–United States–Biography.   I. Title.
BR1725.W433 A3 2001   277.3'083'092–dc21   2001003458

01 02 03 04 05 06—10 9 8 7 6 5 4 3 2 1 0

three years in a row pretty much secured His will for me to stay at home and be a full-time mom for the next season of my life.

Homeschooling is another area in which, given the circumstances, I didn't have a choice, so my heavenly Father made one for me.

Good thing I stumbled into this writing career, because if I had known what I was getting into, I would have run screaming. Graciously, my heavenly Father allowed The Family Dream to come true so that I could continue writing without spending time away from my children.

I have full confidence that God has many other surprises just waiting for me—I have only to turn the corner and discover them.

God has a plan for your life too. I started this book by saying it, and I'm going to end it by saying it: *It is not a coincidence that you are reading this book.* This is you stumbling into the will of God for your life.

God wants to reveal Himself as your heavenly Father. When you're hurting, you can run to Him and crawl up into His lap. When you wonder which way to turn, you can grasp His strong hand, and He'll guide you along life's path. When everything around you is falling apart, you'll feel your Father's arm around your shoulders to hold you together.

If I could convince you of one thing by opening up my life before you, it would be the truth that your heavenly Father loves you beyond comprehension and that He can be trusted with your life—every detail of it.

I recently had a conversation with a gentleman in

Hollywood. He asked me if I would feel comfortable substituting the word *universe* for *God* during my interview. When I said no, he asked me if I could just say *higher power*. I tried to explain to him that my life's message was about the love of God and His power to transform lives through Jesus Christ. I didn't have any personal experience with the "universe" or some impersonal "higher power" that was able to do that. But, I told him, I did have plenty of personal experiences to illustrate the power that's available to him and everyone else through the Creator of the universe—my heavenly Father.

Thank you for allowing me to share some of these personal experiences with you and to brag about my heavenly Father. I just know you'll have plenty of stories of your own to tell when we meet together with our Father in heaven.

Multnomah Publishers ®

The publisher and author would love to hear your comments about this book. *Please contact us at:*
www.multnomah.net/factsoflife

Dedication

With gratitude to the Lord,
I dedicate this book to my three adorable children,
Tucker, Haven, and Clancy.
What a privilege to pass down these stories as a witness to
you and your children of the kind,
trustworthy, and strong hand of our Father in heaven.

Let each generation tell its children
what glorious things he does.

PSALM 145:4, TLB

Table of Contents

A Giant Thank-You Note

I tell my kids, as they grumble that they already *said* thank you, "If someone took the effort to give you a gift, the least you can do is write a thank-you note."

It is my pleasure to write the following collection of thank-you notes to those who have taken the effort to show me their love through the giving of themselves.

Steve,
Thank you for taking the kids to school, cleaning up the dinner dishes, troubleshooting my computer problems, and giving me the kind of love I never have to question.

Love always,
Your adoring wife

Tucker, Haven, and Clancy,
I already said thank you; that should be enough. Just kidding. I appreciate you so much that I dedicated this book to you. And if that's not enough, I also dedicate my life to you. Being your mother is fun.

Love,
Mom

Mama,
I think I finished this book just in time. I'm afraid that a mutiny was around the corner and that my kids were ready to throw me overboard and declare you and Roy captains. Thank you for being not only the best mother in the world but also the best grandmother.

Yours truly,
The best daughter in the world

Daddy,

Thank you for footing the bill for every acting and dance lesson imaginable, a million flights back and forth to Texas, and exorbitant long-distance phone bills. I realize that you gave up more than money for my dreams to come true.

Gratefully,
Your baby girl

Don, Bill, Judith, and all my new friends at Multnomah,
How can I say this without sounding unprofessional? I'm crazy about you guys! You take such good care of me. I respect the way you blend a sense of good business with sensitivity for God's business.

Forever yours (or for at least two more books),
Lisa

Ron,
You continue to amaze me. I'm surprised daily by your expertise, vision, and integrity as a manager. I can't decide whether it's because I had such low expectations of you to begin with or because you really are that good.

Your friend,
Lisa

Jerry and Shirley Grose, Paul and Joy Jones, Tom and Denise McDonald, and Vickie Winner,
I couldn't have written this book without your gracious hospitality. I mean that literally. I tried to write at home, but I failed miserably. Between the kids, e-mail, the phone, the fridge, and the temptation of a nap, there were just too many distractions. Thank you for opening your homes and hearts so wide to me.

Sincerely,
Lisa

Calling all Cyber Prayer Warriors!

Roll call—Deb, Robin, Alice, Curt, Janice, Mick, Mom, Roy, Shawn, Janet, Shirley, Sherilyn, Anastatia, Fred, Denise, Tom, Myrene, Terri, Debby, Andrea, Melissa, Dana, Lynn, Valerie, Gladys, Marie, Jon, JoAnn, Sallie, Connie, Jeannie, Bill, Deb, Gloria, Tammy, Dorothy, Jean, Juanita, Tim, and Cindy. Thank you for carrying this book and me in prayer. You are my own personal band of angels.

In your debt,
Lisa

The Real Facts of Life

I'm so happy that you've picked up this book. I like to think of it as starting a new friendship. With each chapter of my life that I write for you, the closer we can become as friends. I only wish I had a chance to read your life story as well.

To be honest, I don't consider this book an autobiography in the typical this-is-my-whole-life-story sense of the word. I've chosen to delete certain parts of my past; others I've mercifully left out to spare you the boredom; and the future, of course, is yet to be written. But there are a few select stories from my life that I'm thrilled to open up and share with you. That's because the main character isn't me, but my Father.

I was "adopted" by my heavenly Father when I was ten years old. From the day I took His hand as Lord and Savior twenty-eight years ago, He has held on to me for dear life.

And I can't imagine a dearer life than the one I've lived as His child.

An earthly father's role is universally understood to be that of provider and protector. It's also his responsibility to teach his children through both correction and encouragement. Because he is bigger, he can see farther down the road; therefore, when his children look to him, they can find direction for their lives. Best of all, children don't have to earn their daddy's love; it is simply there from the day they are born into his family. This is the relationship I have with my Father in heaven, and I cherish it.

As you read on and our friendship develops, you will understand why I adore Him so. My heavenly Father has taught me many earthly lessons. Make no mistake—God is actively involved in His children's daily lives. In Luke 12, Jesus encourages His disciples and us by saying, "I tell you, don't worry about everyday life—whether you have enough food to eat or clothes to wear. These things dominate the thoughts of most people, but your Father already knows your needs. He will give you all you need from day to day if you make the Kingdom of God your primary concern" (v. 22, 30–31).

I have discovered that my Father in heaven is a detail-oriented God. He is as interested in the little things in our lives as He is in the big things.

He has taught me important life-lessons such as what to learn from failure, when it's good to give up, why He sometimes says no, how to spend money, who to marry, and even where to go when I'm going to blow. These things, I think you'll agree, are the *real* facts of life.

So…how 'bout we grab a piece of cake and a Diet Coke—let's gab a while.

ONE

My Adoption Story

I was born into a fabulous family and had a storybook childhood. My mother was a secretary who devoted her life to being a mother. My younger brother, Cody, was a sweet, fun, strong little boy who ultimately gave up much of his own childhood so that my childhood dreams could come true.

My father, too, sacrificed more than I will ever know. As a little girl, I simply adored him, and now that I'm grown, I still have to have my weekly "daddy fix." If you passed me on the freeway on any given weekend, you'd see me taking advantage of my free weekend minutes to talk with him on my cell phone.

But my Father in heaven is the one I talk to all day long. He's as real to me as my natural father. When I chose to give my life to Jesus as a ten-year-old, I became a child of God—although in John 15:16, Jesus says, "You did not choose me, but I chose you" (NIV). That must be the standard adoptive-parent line. Even if it isn't, it sure makes a child feel special, doesn't it?

Let me tell you my adoption story.

I grew up in a small town in Texas. I was a tomboy and spent my free time climbing trees, riding motorcycles, and playing softball. One Saturday my friend Lynn, who lived a couple of streets over from me, decided that it would be fun to play dress up and go someplace out of the ordinary. Even though I hated wearing dresses, I agreed. I had been the flower girl in my cousin Glenda's wedding and had worn a beautiful, floor-length, hot pink dress. After the ceremony, my mom hemmed the dress to above my knees so I could wear it on special occasions.

Lynn and I decided that going to church would be the perfect out-of-the-ordinary thing to do. You see, although my parents had both been saved as teenagers and loved the Lord, we didn't attend church regularly. I just happened to live two houses down and across the street from a little Baptist church. So it was settled.

The next morning, Lynn and I put on our fancy dresses, hopped on our bicycles, and rode down the street to the neighborhood church. We were directed to the fifth-grade Sunday school class, where we recognized half the kids there from our school. On our way down the hall to the classroom, we passed a pink cardboard box resting on top of a TV tray. I could barely concentrate on being friendly because I couldn't quit staring at the box. I recognized that pink box. It was the same one my daddy would bring home every once in a while for very special mornings. It was a box from the local doughnut shop!

Just after we put together the wooden Jonah-and-the-whale puzzle and right before the flannelboard story about baby Moses in the bulrushes, the teacher brought the box into the room, along with a pitcher of orange juice. There was no longer any question—I caught a whiff of the glazed goodies as the teacher carried them to the back table. Finally, it was snack time! What a treat! My friend Lynn sure had come up with a good idea.

The next Sunday morning I woke up early, took about two seconds to decide whether I wanted toast and jelly or hot, fresh doughnuts for breakfast, and hopped on my bike to head to church again. (This time I didn't mess with wearing a dress.)

Pretty soon I was coming back for more than the doughnuts. I don't know how to explain it, but even at the tender age of ten, I knew that I had found my heart's home. As my Sunday school teacher taught me about Jesus' love for me, I began to fall in love with Him. I didn't really understand what she meant when she told me that He died on the cross to forgive my sins. I certainly had received enough spankings to know that I had sinned, but all I was really sure of was that Jesus was the Son of God and that I wanted Him to live in my heart forever.

That was truly the beginning of my life. Maybe that's why the Bible calls it being born again. I had some sort of understanding that the rest of my life was going to be all about Jesus. Before I ever made it "official" by saying a prayer or walking down the aisle or kneeling at an altar, I was on fire for the Lord.

Every Sunday our class was given a tiny envelope to put our offering in. On the outside was a short checklist. It read like this:

- Read Bible daily.
- Prayed every day.
- Gave an offering.
- Brought a friend to church.

I was diligent all week so that I would be able to check each little box. It's funny how those early habits, formed simply for the thrill of making little check marks on an envelope, have shaped my entire life.

After a while, my parents and little brother began attending church regularly and eventually became very involved in the church. Our family was in charge of the bus ministry. My dad would drive the bus and draw the illustrations for the Bible story. My mom would tell the story. I would entertain with puppets, and six-year-old Cody had fun just riding the bus.

It was at that time that I started going into the "big" church service after Sunday school. As much as I loved the Lord, I remember being extremely bored. My friend Robin and I would pass notes, giggle at the boys, and lie down on the hard pew with our heads on hymnals and fall asleep.

But one Sunday was different. We were all standing, singing the last stanza of the hymn "Just As I Am," when for no apparent reason I began to cry. My mama whispered something into my daddy's ear, and he leaned over and asked me if I wanted to walk down the aisle and give my life to Jesus.

I had no idea what that really meant. I just knew that I had felt the touch of the Lord and that I wanted to respond. When I met the preacher at the front, he led me in a simple prayer asking Jesus to forgive me of my sins and to become the Lord of my life. At that moment my adoption was finalized.

It was years before I understood the full implications of the simple prayer I had repeated. All I knew at that moment was that I was a child of God and that I was willing to go anywhere and do anything my Father asked me to.

So when Jesus tells me, "You did not choose Me, but I chose you," I believe Him. He came looking for me. He devised a plan to get me to church by appealing to my desire to play dress up and do something out of the ordinary. He kept me coming back by offering doughnuts and orange juice, and He drew me into His arms by giving me a supernatural hug.

You know, God is pursuing you too. Do you really think it's just a coincidence that you are reading this book? Whether you realize it or not, God has been wooing you your entire life. He waits patiently for special moments to reveal His love for you. Think back over the many times when you know that your Father reached down from heaven and touched your life. Can you recall instances when you knew He was close beside you, even though you couldn't see Him with your eyes?

You don't have to be able to explain all of these things or even understand them. That ten-year-old girl didn't know why her sins needed to be forgiven, but she did know that she was willing to do whatever it took to make Jesus feel at home in her heart. The next time you sense the heavenly Father drawing near to you, reach out to Him. He simply wants you to respond to Him—like a child.

Two

How I Became an Actress and Then Became Myself

s a little girl I was painfully shy—so much so that when I was seven years old, my mother became concerned. My second grade teacher, Mrs. Clark, had told my mom that I had been helping her in the classroom during recess instead of playing outside with the other kids.

When school let out for the summer, my mom took action. Our public school offered a program for those long, hot, summer Texas days, and you could sign up for any number of fun classes. My mother enrolled me in archery, tumbling, and drama. She had especially high hopes that the acting class would bring me out of my shell.

Her plan was a huge success. By the end of the six-week program, I could hit a bull's-eye and turn a flip—and I had won the lead in the end-of-summer play. I remember what it felt like in the drama class to discover that I was a natural. I felt empowered. When the acting bug bit me, my confidence swelled. It was a defining moment in my life. I decided that I didn't want to wait to become an actress when I grew up—I wanted to be a child-actress.

After the curtain call of our summer production, a lady from the school approached my mother and urged her to sign me up for the professional acting classes that were being offered at the Casa Mañana Playhouse across town in Ft. Worth. I have no idea where my dad found the money or my mom the time, but for the next five years I all but slept at the theater.

I took musical theater, dramatic reading, and mime classes. I studied ballet, tap, and jazz. I acted in children's plays, dinner theater, and summer stock. My theatrical clock was ticking, and I was determined to give birth to a career before I reached puberty.

The first semester of third grade, after my summer acting debut, I auditioned for our school talent show. I couldn't think of any way to use acting as a talent, so I relied on my backup career of tumbling. Basically, I laid out a tumbling mat, put music on the tape recorder, and filled the three-minute song with a series of improvisational flips, cartwheels, and poses. My routine was like the one nearly every little girl performs in her own living room while her daddy stands back and applauds wildly. The applause at school was lackluster at best.

Later that day, when the loudspeaker crackled, I listened eagerly for the principal to announce the names of those who had made it into the talent show. Needless to say, I was crushed when he didn't read my name. Right then, I resolved not only to make it into the talent show next year, but also to win it.

I began work almost immediately. I asked my theater instructor what talent I could perform solo that involved acting. He suggested ventriloquism. I went home and told my mom, and she, as usual, made it happen. She ordered a small ventriloquist figure (you never call them dummies) from the Sears and Roebuck catalog. The puppet came with an instructional record and booklet. After the package arrived, I practiced almost every day, teaching myself how to speak without moving my lips. Eventually, "The doy dounced the dasketdall" began sounding more and more like "The boy bounced the basketball."

All the hard work paid off when, as a fourth grader, I won first place in the Lake Worth Public School Talent Show. I figured that I was about to fulfill my heart's desire to become a child-actress and that I was on my way to stardom.

But, ironically, my mother's original intent to draw me out of my shyness was never realized. Even though I had found my niche as an actress, it didn't translate into confidence on the playground. I was still a bookworm who felt more comfortable in a corner reading than joining in with the other kids.

Not until I was in my midtwenties did I discover that God created me with an extroverted personality. He never intended for me to be shy. Shyness was a defense mechanism I had put up as a small child. Who knows why, but I felt safer keeping to myself than risking getting hurt by other people. And I kept that shield up for years.

I remember that as a young adult I wanted desperately to be a part of a small prayer group, but I felt so suffocated by insecurity that I could barely speak, much less pray. I recall recoiling every time someone approached me on the street for an autograph—not because I was snobby, but because I was afraid to let a stranger in. I hated parties because small talk was unbearable for me. As long as I was with my mother, a best friend, or acting, I was fine; but introduce me to someone I didn't know and I froze up. I accepted it as "just the way I am" and continued to live in my shell, venturing out only when I knew it was absolutely safe.

Then one day I was set free. I had made an appointment with a pastor at our church for counseling regarding another matter (I can't even remember what it was now). While we were praying, he stopped, looked at me, and said, "Lisa, God really loves you." I knew that. By then, I had been a Christian for fifteen years.

But God was trying to teach me something deeper. Suddenly I understood that I had spent my life trying to be perfect in every way—first by trying to earn my parents' love and then my heavenly Father's. But because we can never be good enough to deserve God's love, I always felt as if I were failing Him, so I tried harder, never learning how to rest in His love. I confessed this to my pastor: "I know that God loves me, but I don't *feel* as though He loves me."

It shocked me when he responded rather sternly, "God's love is not a feeling; it is who He is. You must make a choice: Either you believe Him and accept His love, or you believe your feelings and reject Him." That was an eye opener.

Accepting God's love as a gift instead of trying to earn it had somehow seemed presumptuous and arrogant to me, when, in fact, my pride was tricking me into thinking that I could merit His love and forgiveness with my own strength. At that moment something clicked inside me, and I made the choice to believe that God had made me "good enough" the day I accepted His Son's death on the cross as punishment for all my failures—not only the mistakes in my past, but also those I would surely make in the future.

What freedom!

I no longer had to work so hard to try to be perfect. At that time, I also must have realized that if my Father in heaven loved me just the way I was, I didn't need to fear rejection from people. Months later it dawned on me that I no longer felt the gripping panic I had grown so accustomed to when meeting new people. In small groups I became funny, talkative, and interested in reaching out to other people. In fact, now I have to be careful not to "interview" people to death or cross that fine line between extroverted and obnoxious.

It still amazes me to realize that I was once so bound by fear of rejection that I couldn't even recognize myself. It's even more amazing to me that my lifelong habit of self-protection was broken the instant I chose to believe that God really loved me as much as He said He did, whether I felt that He did or not.

Do you feel that God loves you? It doesn't matter. He does. He says so in Romans 8:39: "Whether we are high above the sky or in the deepest ocean, nothing in all creation will ever be able to separate us from the love of God that is revealed in Christ Jesus our Lord."

Nothing you have ever done or will ever do can make Him love you any less. For that matter, nothing you will ever do can make Him love you any more. Believing that you are loved will set you free to be who God created you to be.

So rest in His love and just be yourself. You may be surprised at who you really are.

THREE

The Proverbial Stage Father

*T*hey say that behind every child-actress is a stage mother. Well, in my case, it was a stage Father. God has been living His life through me since I was a little girl.

God has been both my manager and my agent. He's been at every lesson, audition, and performance, cheering me on and directing me from backstage. I know that's the case because nothing but His sovereign will for my life could have brought me this far. My very first job in show business is a perfect illustration.

When I was twelve years old, my mother read in *TV Guide* that Walt Disney Productions was going to revive the *Mickey Mouse Club* and that the studio was going to conduct a nationwide talent search for twelve new mouseketeers. I was so excited. I just knew that they would have auditions in

Dallas and that I would have the chance to fulfill my dream of becoming a child-actress.

So I was devastated when a few months later my mom read an article that said that Disney Studios had auditioned more than six thousand kids and were down to final callbacks for the new show. How could this have happened? Had they come through Texas without my hearing about it? Being a stuck-up Texan, I never considered the possibility that they might have skipped the Lone Star state altogether.

Knowing how disappointed I was, my mom came up with a plan. One Saturday we went to her office, and I wrote letters to every acting teacher, stage director, and Kiwanis Club leader who had ever seen me perform. I asked each one to write a letter of reference on my behalf to the casting director at Walt Disney Productions. The idea was to bombard the studio with letters about Lisa Whelchel so they would think, *Gosh, it sounds like we'd better give this girl a chance.*

In addition, I wrote a personal letter of appeal to the casting director. I made it clear that my daddy had agreed to fly me to California at his own expense if they would let me audition. I went on to explain that I didn't want to wait until I was grown up to become an actress. I wanted to be an actress *now,* and Walt Disney Studios was the perfect place for me to realize my dream. I ended the letter by saying that I was a Christian and that, given the climate of television and movie roles for young girls these days, there didn't seem to be very many prospects for me in show business that wouldn't compromise my beliefs. I couldn't let this opportunity pass me by.

Mom's ingenious plan worked. One evening we received a call from Los Angeles. If I could be in California the following week, they would give me a chance to audition. The next few days were a whirlwind. I took private tap dancing lessons to learn a quick dance routine. (Dancing was not my strong suit.) I practiced singing and playing "You've Got a Friend" on my guitar until my fingers were raw. And I talked more with my mouth closed than with it open as I rehearsed my ventriloquism routine.

The big day finally arrived. My mother and I caught our first flight, took our first cab ride, and stayed in our first hotel room—all on the same day. We were so naive that we spent the first night sightseeing up and down Hollywood Boulevard—alone. Thank God for guardian angels.

When I walked into a rehearsal studio the day of my audition, a handful of producers were lined up along the mirrored wall. I launched into my ventriloquism routine, but that was the only thing they allowed me to finish. Next I sang a song, but they cut me off in the middle and asked me to show them a tap-shuffle-ball-change. The only other thing they asked me to do before I left was to pretend that I was eating a banana.

Pretend to eat a banana? I was so deflated. How could I face my friends at home? Would my daddy think that he'd wasted all that money? And was my dream of becoming a child-actress just a fantasy?

Years later, I discovered what happened that day. One of the producers told my mother that they all knew I had the part within the first five minutes of my audition. From that point, they didn't care if I could dance or sing or play the guitar. They had seen enough and knew that I was what they were looking for in a mouseketeer.

Of course, I didn't know any of this, so I was shocked when my mother woke me up a week later to tell me that the casting director from Walt Disney Studios was on the phone and wanted to talk to me. A few months later, I left home to begin my career as a child-actress.

It never crossed my mind that I was leaving home for good. My mother now says that she regrets ever having encouraged me to write those letters. She just wanted to be a good mother and help her daughter fulfill her heart's desire. She didn't realize that it would be the last time I would call Texas my home. But ultimately my mother wasn't in charge of my life; my heavenly Father was, and He had other plans for me.

There is something incredibly comforting about knowing that the Creator is in control of your life. It means that if you have a dream—no matter how impossible it may seem to you now—if you've let God in on it, He can move heaven and earth to make it happen.

Psalm 37:4–5 says, "Take delight in the LORD, and he will give you your heart's desires. Commit everything you do to the LORD. Trust him, and he will help you." The key words are *delight, commit,* and *trust.* If you truly delight in the Lord and His ways, your desires will be closer to His desires. And you can sincerely commit your heart's dreams to Him if you trust Him.

What is your heart's desire? Is it something the Lord

would be delighted to give you? Do you trust Him enough to commit it to Him? God is able to make it happen. Life as a child of God means that you can hold on to your dreams and give them to Him at the same time. So hold on to your dreams knowing that your heavenly Father is holding on to you.

FOUR

It's Only a Part

*B*eing a mouseketeer on *The New Mickey Mouse Club* was the role of a lifetime. We taped 186 song-and-dance-filled episodes, performed live stage shows at Disneyland, and rode on giant mouse-ear floats in the Disney World Main Street parade. What a great profession!

But they don't call it show business for nothing. For reasons I still don't understand, the show was canceled, and at thirteen years old I was out of a job.

I got an agent in California and began looking for work. My mom continued to hop back and forth between Texas and California, trying to raise two children in two different states. When she was home, I had various guardians who stayed with me. Eventually my grandmother, Nanny, came to live with me most of the time.

For a couple of years, I guest starred on television shows and in several movies that went straight to video. Then in 1979, when I was sixteen, a casting director called my agent and said that they had a part that was perfect for me. The role was written for a character named Blair, a fast-talking, naive girl from Texas, in a show that was called *Garrett's Girls*. It was a pilot for a spin-off of the NBC show *Different Strokes*.

When I auditioned for the role, I read a certain line in the script rather condescendingly while looking down disdainfully at the rump of the girl beside me. Weeks later, when I showed up for the first day of rehearsal, I was surprised to see that Blair's character had been rewritten to match my reading of that one line. So I guess I'm to blame for Blair's less than humble personality.

But wait—I'm getting ahead of myself. Before I got the role of Blair, I had been offered another role on a series that was already on the air. The show was *Hello Larry*, starring MacLean Stevenson, and they needed to replace the actress who played the older sister.

That was a tough decision. Should I go for the sure thing, the show that was already on the air? Or should I go for the fun thing, the great character on a pilot episode that might never make it to series? Thankfully, I was too stupid to pick the safe bet—or perhaps it was God acting as my manager again. I chose *The Facts of Life*, and the rest is television history.

At the beginning of each season, a small group of writers and producers would sit down with the cast and discuss the upcoming episodes they were writing. The first meeting of this kind was at the beginning of the second season. Someone needed to enlighten us as to why our original cast had dwindled from seven girls to three over the summer vacation.

They explained that there were too many girls to get to know in a thirty-minute time slot, so they had trimmed the cast, leaving Natalie, Tootie, and Blair. They had also added a character, Jo, to foil Blair. Nancy McKeon was such a delightful addition to the cast that it took some of the sting out of losing so many new friends.

The meeting before the third season was traumatic for me. We were casually told that the network had decided that they couldn't have a show entitled *The Facts of Life* and not deal with that particular issue.

The producers went on to explain that Blair would lose her virginity in an episode to be aired during sweeps week— when the networks air their most attention-grabbing shows in order to get higher ratings and, thus, higher advertising rates.

I don't remember much else of what was said during that meeting. My mind was reeling as I tried to figure out how I was going to deal with this new situation. The show was still early in its run, and I wasn't really in a position to question the producers. But I knew I couldn't compromise my beliefs either.

When the meeting ended, I lingered so I could speak with the producers privately. I explained that I felt a responsibility to the young girls who might be watching the show. Some of them might be thinking about losing their virginity and feel tempted to bow to peer pressure by saying, "See, everyone's doing it, even Blair."

Unlike in a television sitcom, that kind of life decision cannot be made and then resolved in seventeen minutes before the final commercial break. The consequences, regardless of the outcome, impact a person's life forever. Once a girl gives away her virginity, she can never get it back. God created sex, and He instructs His children to wait until marriage to enjoy it. I certainly didn't want to go on television and by my actions say, "God doesn't know what He's talking about. Having premarital sex is a normal, healthy fact of life."

The producers tried to convince me that it was only a part, that it wasn't really me. But I could see the big picture and stood firm (actually I was trembling). Ultimately, they respected my beliefs, and the episode wasn't written—at least, not until the last season of the show when the ratings were lagging and another sweeps week was around the corner. This time they knew better than to approach me, so they wrote the episode around Natalie.

In the original script for that episode, Blair was to take a stand for abstinence. That was extremely gracious of the producers, but I requested to be written out of the episode altogether. Although it would have been a wonderful opportunity to share the truth about the value of waiting for marriage to have sex, it would have been offered as just another option, not as God's perfect plan. I realized that the overall message of the show would perpetuate the lie that having sex before marriage is natural, with no negative consequences as long as people practice "safe sex."

The producers, once again, granted my request. Because I had asked to be written out, I assumed that I would not be paid for the episode. My salary at that time was fifty-five thousand dollars per episode, but I was happy to pay whatever price to stand up for what I believed.

I was especially thankful for the opportunity to stand up for my beliefs because I hadn't always made the best choices earlier in my career. I bought into the rationalization that "It's only a part." For instance, I regret that even though it wasn't a real cigarette, I gave the impression in the first episode of *The Facts of Life* that Blair smoked. I'm embarrassed by some of the immodest clothing I wore in a few of the television movies I was in. And I can't believe I once accepted a part in a movie without ever reading the rest of the script. My role was harmless enough, but the rest of the movie was awful.

As I grow as a child of the Lord, my discernment concerning the parts I will take as an actress has grown as well. But it's such a relief to know that my Father understands that, as children, before we learn to walk, we crawl. And before we can stand up for what we believe, we may fall down a few times.

The apostle Paul said it best:

It's like this: When I was a child, I spoke and thought and reasoned as a child does. But when I grew up, I put away childish things. (1 Corinthians 13:11)

The Lord hasn't condemned me for the poor choices I made when I was younger. He knows me completely, and He understands that I didn't know any better at the time. As I grow in the Lord and am able to see things more clearly, He expects me to make better choices, and I'll continue to obey according to the glimpses of truth I'm given.

Have you ever made a poor choice? Of course you have. That's like asking a baby, "Have you ever made a mess in your diaper?" Of course he has. Don't be so hard on yourself—God isn't yelling at you. Your heavenly Father is saying to you gently, "Let Me clean you up, and then let Me train you."

God knows that children have a learning curve. He also understands that even His little ones who know better will occasionally have "accidents." That's not to say that He will have the same reaction now as He will ten years from now. God judges our hearts, and He is the only one who knows what can be expected of us as His children.

So be careful: Don't be so hard on yourself, and even more important, don't be too hard on others. You can't see their hearts, and remember, we're all still growing by glimpses. You may think you can see the big picture, but in this case, it *is* only a part.

FIVE

I'm Not Watching My Weight: Everyone Else Is

I t was so much fun playing Blair on *The Facts of Life*. In fact, I'm more than a little embarrassed to admit how easy it was to play that part. People ask me all the time if I'm anything like Blair in real life.

First of all, there's no way my mama would allow me to act like Blair. Second, Blair and I don't look or sound alike: I have a remnant of a Texas twang, and Blair is from New York. She's also much taller than me. At five feet three, I'm vertically challenged. The funny thing is that all the other girls on the show were even shorter, but Blair wore high heels all the time, so next to them she looked like a giant. That's another difference—I wear tennis shoes 90 percent of the time. Blair's and my wardrobes are totally different. When I get dressed in the morning, *comfort* is the operative word. I doubt that Blair would feel the same way.

There is, however, one obvious similarity between Blair

and me. We both struggle with our weight. At the mall, girls still approach me and say, "Blair! You don't look as fat as you do on TV!" (Am I supposed to say thank you?)

Adolescence, for me, was a cruel "fact of life." Unfortunately, someone forgot to tell me that a television star isn't allowed to go through puberty, or that if she does she had better hide it, especially if she's been cast—as I was—to play a perennially beautiful, rich, thin ingénue.

I began packing on the pounds toward the end of the second season. Let me tell you how it happened: At the end of the first season, the actors' union went on strike, which meant that production was completely shut down until negotiations were completed. I headed back home to Texas to wait it out. With both the strike and our production hiatus, I was home for more than six months—and it turned out to be one of the happiest times of my life.

Since leaving Texas in the sixth grade, I had been tutored on various sets and done my schoolwork independently at home. (I guess I was homeschooled before homeschooling was cool.) Now I was sixteen, and I enrolled at a Christian high school so that I could double up on my work and graduate before I returned to Los Angeles.

For the first time in four years, I was living at home with my family. I was going to football games, dating, and making friends. My daddy bought me a brand-new gold Pontiac Trans Am with a T-top and an awesome stereo system. My girlfriends and I would pop in an eight-track (yeah, I know, I'm old), and we would drive around Ft. Worth singing at the top of our lungs.

I also got involved in the youth group at my church. We would have Bible study pizza parties or "Asteroids" tournaments at the local submarine sandwich shop/arcade and then pile into my car and head to the neighborhood Dairy Queen drive-thru for cookies-and-cream blizzards. I was in hog heaven (no pun intended).

You know the saying that all good things must come to an end? No one warned me that the end would be so apocalyptic. Within a short period of time, my parents filed for divorce, my church split down the middle, and the actors' strike was settled. No more family, no more school, and no more friends. All I had left was my job.

Or did I?

The first day back at work it was obvious to the producers that I had visited the Dairy Queen drive-thru on my way to just about everywhere and that I had done a bit more pizza eating than Bible studying. Millions of dollars were riding on Blair looking a certain way. Consequently, although my plight was understandable, there was very little room for compassion. The producers made it quite clear that I would lose either the weight or my job.

They swooped down on me like a lonely girl on a carton of ice cream. They hired nutritionists, therapists, and hypnotists. They sent me to fat farms, exercise trainers, and health spas. They even brought the scale to the rehearsal hall and had me weigh in every morning, while everyone gathered round to see if I had gained or lost any weight.

I don't blame them for any of the measures they took. They were doing their jobs; I was *not* doing mine. I didn't fulfill my end of the contract. They had hired me to fill a particular role, and I filled it to overflowing. Still—human nature being what it is—the more they pushed, the more I ate.

A few images are emblazoned in my memory. One is of me walking down an aisle in the grocery store, checking expiration dates for the freshest chocolate pastry and then eating it before I got to the checkout stand. I also remember sneaking out of a fat farm to take an afternoon hike—to the candy store in town to devour a can of Almond Roca. The ugliest memory is of me leaning over the toilet in a Chinese restaurant trying desperately to make myself throw up because I had eaten too much and was afraid that I would lose my job.

Clearly, I was hungry—but not for food.

Finally, when I was at my lowest point, a friend asked me a question that changed my life. "Lisa, you sound miserable," he said. "How much time are you spending with the Lord?"

I raised my eyebrows. "Well, I pray every day," I said. "I read my Bible every night before I go to bed, and I go to church every Sunday."

"I don't mean what you're *doing* for the Lord—I mean how much time are you spending just being with Him and getting to know Him?" He gestured at the two of us. "You know...like friends do."

I wrinkled my brow in thought and then admitted weakly, "I guess not very much."

"Why don't you try a new diet?" he asked. "You can eat anything you want for the next two weeks. The only stipulation is that you must set your alarm every morning and spend time with God before you go to work."

I nodded, eager to try it. This was the best diet I'd ever heard of—and I thought I had tried them all. For the next fourteen days, as soon as I woke up every morning, I went into the bathroom. (I lived in a studio apartment with my grandmother, and it was the only room where I could turn on the light and not wake her.) I closed the door, grabbed my Bible, and sat on the pot (with the lid down!). Some days, I would read God's Word and feel as if He was speaking directly to me. Other times, I felt so bored that I could barely keep my eyes open. But I knew that my time with my Father was feeding my soul.

I also spent time in prayer, picturing Jesus sitting beside me, on the rim of the bathtub. Often I started my talks with God by saying, "I love You." Then I spilled everything: how much I missed my family, how I wished I could go home, how I wanted to find a girlfriend in California, how sorry I was that I'd failed so many people. As I prayed, the pangs of loneliness and hunger began to subside, and I discovered the truth of Jesus' promise: "I am the bread of life. No one who comes to me will ever be hungry again" (John 6:35).

My favorite part of the "diet" was the time I spent sitting quietly, just being with Jesus. I wouldn't say anything, and most of the time He wouldn't either. Sometimes I even fell asleep. But I knew that He was there. I could sense His presence, and it filled the emptiness in my soul.

My life turned around during those two weeks, and it has never been the same since. Physically I stayed the same (I wish I could say I suddenly dropped twenty pounds and never had to count another calorie, but I can't), but on the inside I was different. Over time, my hormones evened out, and I lost the baby fat. But before that happened, I lost the emptiness I had been trying to fill with food.

Food is just one of the ways we attempt to find satisfaction apart from relationship with our heavenly Father. Some people get drunk every weekend in an effort to quench their thirsty souls. You won't catch me pointing a finger and asking, "How could you?" I understand. For a while the emptiness inside you seems to go away. Unfortunately, it always comes back.

Or maybe you don't give that emptiness a chance to come back. At the first pang of reality you reach for your drug of choice because it's just too painful not to be high. There are less obvious drugs. Have you ever tried shopping? That works almost as well as trying to drown out the hunger by turning up your stereo full blast.

Most of us are content to live with the hunger as long as it's only temporary. We assume that as soon as we get married the yearning will subside. Or maybe we're counting on popularity or success to make the cravings go away. If we just had more money, we would finally be full. But I had what the world would consider "having it all," and I was still starving.

Only an ongoing relationship with Jesus can fill that emptiness in your soul. Jesus said, "People need more than bread for their life; they must feed on every word of God" (Matthew 4:4).

May I ask you a question? How much time are you spending with the Lord every day? Tomorrow morning I'm going to get up before everyone else in my family does and feed on the Lord (John 6:57, NIV). Why don't you join me? It's always easier to start a new diet with a friend.

SIX

Thorn in the Excess Flesh

I wish you could see a picture of me as a baby. I would have made a perfect Gerber baby. Not because I was so cute, but because it was obvious that I had eaten a lot of Gerber baby food! My thighs looked like those wiener dogs that balloon artists make and sell at the fair. It was hard to tell where the thigh ended and the calf began. Actually, they weren't calves at all—they were full-grown cows.

I ballooned most dramatically during my teens, but I always struggled with my weight. When I was eleven, I was already full-figured. I remember the trauma of not being able to fit into the popular jeans like Dittos or Luv-its. Everyone wore them—except me. I wore Wranglers.

But when I arrived in Hollywood, my weight became a bigger issue than whether I could squeeze into a pair of Wrangler slims. The question of dieting first came up while I was rehearsing a production number for *The New Mickey*

Mouse Club. The choreographer walked by, patted my belly, and commented, "That's quite a little gut you got on ya, kid."

The next day I started my first diet, and I continued dieting for three years. Then, when I was fifteen, my inability to lose weight at a normal rate landed me in the hospital—not because I was sick, but because I was so well. Amazed at my "superefficient" body, the doctors admitted me to a diagnostic hospital in Galveston, Texas, where I spent two weeks undergoing tests and experiments. Beginning with 1500 calories a day and lowering that intake every three days, they determined that my basal metabolic rate was 600 calories a day. That meant I didn't lose weight until they fed me three scrumptious meals that added up to 400 calories. If I had lived in caveman days, I would have been legendary.

Twenty years ago it wasn't clear why I couldn't lose weight, but with recent health discoveries, it's obvious. I had been dieting and exercising strenuously since I was twelve years old, and my body had gone into famine mode. My body had been starving for so long that it was hoarding every calorie as if it were the last.

I have only recently come to equate my struggle with my weight as a "thorn in the flesh." The apostle Paul writes in the New Testament:

> I have plenty to boast about and would be no fool in doing it, because I would be telling the truth. But I won't do it. I don't want anyone to think more highly of me than what they can actually see in my life and

my message, even though I have received wonderful revelations from God. But to keep me from getting puffed up, I was given a thorn in my flesh, a messenger from Satan to torment me and keep me from getting proud. Three different times I begged the Lord to take it away. Each time he said, "My gracious favor is all you need. My power works best in your weakness." (2 Corinthians 12:6–9)

I have experienced many blessings from the Lord and have been given much that I could boast about. My weight struggle has served not only to keep me humble, but it has also been an issue that allows me to identify with so many other women who might otherwise be tempted to think more highly of me than I deserve. I've asked the Lord many times to help me lose weight, but so far His answer has been no.

And I've done my part! For instance, early last year I was determined to lose the twenty pounds I had put on since getting married and having babies. I bought the bestselling *Body for Life* and joined a local gym with my mom and two close girlfriends. You'll know what close friends they really are when I tell you that we took "before" pictures of each other in bathing suits. (I kept the negatives for blackmail just in case I get into financial trouble years from now.)

In two and a half months I missed only three days of working out. I looked downright buff. I was drinking plaster of Paris shakes and eating healthy stuff like The Emperor's New Protein Bars—you know, the "make 'em look like a candy bar and see if anybody notices that they're really doggie treats" bars. When it came time for me to take my "after" pictures, I had lost *one* pound, and my muscle-to-fat ratio hadn't changed *a single* percentage point. Can you believe those results? I was deflated emotionally, but physically I hadn't let any air out of my spare tire.

I would be tempted to try another fad diet except that I've already tried enough of them to know that they are a waste of time. Sure, I lose weight, but I always gain it back—with interest.

I once tried taking a shortcut, when my doctor prescribed the latest diet pills, Phen-Fen. They worked for a while, but my heavenly Father made it very clear to me that He didn't want me going that route. He used the illustration of the children of Israel to teach me: The Lord had promised to deliver the Israelites from their enemies, but they couldn't wait on Him to do it their way or on their timetable, so they asked Egypt for military help. God said, "Destruction is certain for those who look to Egypt for help, trusting their cavalry and chariots instead of looking to the LORD, the Holy One of Israel" (Isaiah 31:1). I knew that that was a warning to me, so I flushed the diet pills down the toilet.

But, as children are wont to do, I looked for a loophole. Surely God didn't mean the all-natural, homeopathic metabolism boosters sold in health stores, for goodness' sake. So I tried the herbal diet pills. I'm so glad that God is in control of my life. He made this choice easy. I could either take the pills, stay up twenty-four hours straight, have a continual light-strobe display in my right eye, and nearly faint every time I stood up quickly—*or* I could obey Him all the way and not even think about phoning Egypt for help. So I flushed the herbal diet pills down the toilet too. (The toilet has lost a lot of weight—but it's probably just water.)

I have to confess: It sure is tough to trust the Lord to win the battles for you when you always seem to be losing—or, as in my case, not losing. By everyday standards, I'm an average-to-fluffy-size woman for my age group. And I wouldn't mind the extra fluff that much if I didn't know that I'm judged by a different standard because I'm on television. Compare me to any of the ladies on *Friends,* and suddenly my extra cushion seems like a queen-size mattress.

For the last ten years I've been able to hide out in suburbia in elastic-waist pants and oversize tops. But the time has come for me to venture beyond my comfort zone. ABC television will soon begin filming a *Facts of Life* reunion special. I have to lose at least ten pounds or face the inevitable critical reviews depicting Blair as the beauty queen all the women want to rub elbows with at the high school reunion because they are secretly thrilled that she has gotten fat.

As soon as the contracts for the special were negotiated, I headed for the gym, and for two months I have pumped iron twice a week. On the other days I'm either kickboxing, spinning, or stepping. I've given up desserts, and I'm eating a healthy diet. Guess what? I haven't lost a single pound.

I would be lying if I told you that I'm not scared. I don't want to face the insults. I understand that Hollywood has set a standard that is not even close to reality, and I realize that most people in America are not superthin. But I have also been in this business long enough to know what America expects people to look like on television.

Thankfully, I have been in this relationship with the Lord even longer than I've been in show business. I've seen Him do miracles in my life. If He wants me to lose ten pounds, it's easy for Him to do. If He says no, I can say with Paul, "Since I know it is all for Christ's good, I am quite content with my weaknesses and with insults, hardships, persecutions, and calamities. For when I am weak, then I am strong" (2 Corinthians 12:10).

I don't know how this is all going to turn out, but I do know that I can trust the Lord. He will win this battle one way or the other. He probably won't ride up on horse and chariot; He might not even show up as early as I'd like Him to. But I will wait for Him, for He is faithful.

I believe that God allows each of us our own "thorn in the flesh"—that thing in our lives that we can't seem to beat no matter how hard we try. I'm not suggesting that you should give up or give in. Personally, I will continue to fight all my life to stay at a healthy weight. But I *am* recommending that you look to the Lord for your strength and thank Him for the thorn. Why?

- Because there's something about not being able to be in control that makes it easier to give God control.
- Because we're more likely to give God the glory for triumphs when we have tried in our strength and failed.
- Because it's a natural progression to our knees when we're getting up from a fall.

- Because if life were trouble-free, we would never call on the Lord and would miss out on the thrill of being rescued.

Are you tired of trying and failing? Then cry out to the Lord in your despair. He might not remove the thorn, but He will stand beside you. If the thorn is in your foot, He will carry you. If the thorn is in your hand, He will lend His. If the thorn is in your head, He will remind you of the crown of thorns He wore for you.

In your greatest weakness, turn to your greatest strength—Jesus—and hear Him say, "My grace is sufficient for you, for My strength is made perfect in weakness" (2 Corinthians 12:9, NKJV).

SEVEN

His Name Is Wonderful Financial Counselor

My daughter, Haven, regularly says to me, "Tell me something bad you did when you were a little girl." She can listen to the same stories over and over again and never tire of them. So I tell her about a time when my parents were playing cards with the neighbors. They had sent us kids to our rooms to play. Back then kids were to be seen and not heard—except in this case we weren't even to be seen. I got bored while we played board games, so I poked out all the little picture windows on the View-Master slides.

They say that you store those memories from your childhood that had the most impact on your life. That must be true because I have never forgotten the impact my mother had on my bottom when she found that broken toy.

"Tell me another one," Haven begs. So I tell her about being the only student in my school to win the President's

Physical Fitness Award when I was in sixth grade. My mother brags about that accomplishment to this day. That's why I never told anyone, until Haven asked, that I cheated.

We were assigned partners to count how many chin-ups we could do in a minute. I got tired halfway through and put my feet on the ground. After a few seconds rest, I hopped back up to the bar and finished the requisite number. My friend never snitched. There were a dozen other criteria that I completed fair and square, but because I cheated on that one, I've never been able to enjoy the victory or wear the award patch they gave me.

Her favorite story is the one where I was at the Six Flags over Texas amusement park with the youth group from church. We were driving the little Autopia cars around the track, and I stopped mine in the middle of the ride, hopped out, jumped the bush, and abandoned it there. Isn't that terrible!

I was a pretty good kid, but I definitely had a mischievous streak. I was almost cured of it the night my friend Michelle and I played the "purse trick" at my Nanny's house out in the country. We got an old purse and tied some fishing line to it and waited until it got dark and laid it out beside the two-lane road. We strung out the fishing line and hid in the bushes a few yards away.

The object of the trick was to get somebody to drive past the purse, become intrigued, and pull over. Then when they got close to it we would drag it into the bushes. The person would look everywhere before concluding that they were just seeing things. They would drive off and we would stumble out of the dark, laughing our heads off as we prepared for our next prey.

But one night we were the prey—and boy did we pray! This particular victim was drunk and was not amused. We could hear the expletives, but all we could see of him was his lighted cigarette—heading toward us. When he got close enough for us to smell whiskey, Michelle and I jumped up and tore off across the pasture. I never looked back. And although I was looking ahead of me, it was too dark to see anything—which is why I ran full force into a barbed wire fence and flipped over it, leaving shreds of my shorts and flesh behind.

I don't mind telling Haven these stories. It makes her feel better to know that she's not the only one who has ever done something bad. And perhaps she'll learn from my mischief and mistakes. Lord knows, some of the most important lessons I've ever learned were ones He taught me through my failures. Maybe by listening to my stories, Haven won't make some of the same mistakes I've made. That's why I want to tell you about one of the times I disobeyed the Lord and the life-changing lesson I learned from it.

When I was eighteen years old, I attended The Praise Gathering, an event hosted annually by the gospel music team of Bill and Gloria Gaither. Dr. Tony Campolo, a sociologist and a dynamic speaker, gave the evening message. As he told stories about the thousands of starving children in Haiti, my eyes were opened to what a privileged life I lived and how totally unaware I was of what was going on in the rest of the world.

I was profoundly moved and convicted. At the end of the message, I approached Dr. Campolo and, sobbing, dropped my Rolex watch and diamond and emerald ring into his coat pocket. I asked him to sell them and give the money to help the poor.

But this was more than a moment of emotion stirred up by an anointed preacher. Now that my eyes had been opened, I couldn't close them and pretend that I hadn't seen anything. I was responsible to do something with this new information.

When I got back to L.A., I sat down at my kitchen table and came up with a plan. I could easily live on 10 percent of my salary. I decided to sell my condominium and rent a nice apartment. It wasn't necessary for a single girl to live in a three-bedroom, two-story condo. And I certainly didn't need to be driving around in a Porsche. Selling the car and buying a moderate car would free up thousands of dollars. I had money invested in real estate across the country. If I sold it, the money would feed tens of thousands of children. It was a no-brainer.

My zeal was strong. I knew that I had heard from God and that I was doing the right thing. The tough part was convincing my mother, my manager, and my accountant. Understandably, they thought I was caught up in momentary feelings of guilt and compassion.

They were fine with my tithing and giving occasional offerings, but they thought my plan was irrational. As I tried to implement it, weeks turned into months, and my resolve began to break down under the weight of their arguments, which seemed full of logic and wisdom. Eventually I abandoned the call, closed my eyes, and returned blindly to living a life that seemed to make sense.

But God doesn't always make sense, at least not on this side of things. He had told me, as He had once told His disciples:

> "Sell what you have and give to those in need. This will store up treasure for you in heaven! And the purses of heaven have no holes in them. Your treasure will be safe—no thief can steal it and no moth can destroy it. Wherever your treasure is, there your heart and thoughts will also be." (Luke 12:33–34)

As it turned out, what seemed foolish in the eyes of the world was wisdom from the Lord's perspective. Less than ten years later, all that money was gone anyway. A chunk of it had been invested in a high-rise office building in Pittsburgh that went belly-up. Another significant portion was in Texas land that dried up during the oil crisis and was eventually foreclosed upon. When I got married, I sold my condo and bought a house during the California real estate boom in the 1980s, only to have to give it back to the bank three years later when the bottom fell out of the market. *The Facts of Life* was canceled, and I spent all the cash I had making payments on everything for as long as I could. At twenty-eight, I was broke.

That's when I realized that God's ways do make sense. He could see farther down the road than I could—or, for that matter, than my mother, manager, or accountant could. He was trying to get me to invest my money in heaven, where it would be safe, but I thought it was too risky to take Him at His word. Sometimes the things God asks us to do seem unwise, illogical, or unrealistic:

- Be happy about it when you are made fun of for following Jesus (Matthew 5:11–12).
- Don't worry about your life (Matthew 6:25).
- If someone slaps you on the cheek, offer the other one as well (Matthew 5:39).
- Be willing to forgive your enemy seventy times seven (Matthew 18:22).
- You are to be perfect, even as your Father in heaven is perfect (Matthew 5:48).
- Don't have sex before marriage (Ephesians 5:3).

In comparison, "Sell what you have and give it to those in need" sounds reasonable. Are you willing to take God at His word even if everything and everyone around you tells you to stick with what makes sense?

Let's consider a tragic illustration: John Kennedy Jr.'s plane crash into the Atlantic Ocean. The official report said that it was pilot error due to spatial disorientation. From what I understand, a pilot is more likely to experience this sensation when he is over the water on hazy, moonless nights when it's harder to see the horizon.

In those circumstances, the pilot has to stop relying on what he can see because there is no dependable point of reference and he's basically flying blind. At the same time, he must resist trusting his instincts, especially while making adjustments, or he runs the risk of overcompensating and heading into a "death spiral." The only way to survive this situation is to rely solely and completely on the airplane's instruments to guide it to a safe landing.

The Lord is our point of reference, but there will be dark, hazy nights when we can't see Him and can't figure out in which direction we are heading. There will be times in our lives when we can't trust our senses and aren't able to make decisions depending on whether something makes sense or not. Our only chance for survival is to go back to what will never change—His Word. God can see clearly no matter how dark or foggy the night is. Trust His Word to guide you safely home. It may feel risky, but in reality, it will save you from losing everything.

EIGHT

"Shear" Grace

The years I spent filming *The Facts of Life* were loaded with fun (especially seasons seven and eight, when George Clooney was around). They don't make shows like that anymore. And from what I hear from my friends who are still in the television industry, sitcom sets like the one I was privileged to work on for nine years are rare.

The cast, crew, and production staff were like a family, and the girls were like my sisters, which meant that there were equal amounts of fighting and laughing. But laughter always won in the end. The writers, producers, and directors didn't mind our practical jokes and horsing around because they knew that come taping day we would settle down and be professional.

Nevertheless, I had to learn that it was important to be

professional even during rehearsals. The other girls were tutored in the school trailer four hours a day, but since I was a couple of years older than they were and had graduated early, I was on the set all day. Therefore, I had lots more rehearsal time.

By day two, I would have my lines and blocking down cold, so I would coast until tape day. I was never without a good book, and it wasn't unusual for me to read during a scene. I would take my eyes from the page just long enough to say my lines, and then I would get back to my book. I didn't see a problem with this because I rarely missed a cue, and besides it was only rehearsal.

So I was shocked when one afternoon Nancy, Mindy, and Kim came to my dressing room quite upset. I laid my book on the couch and invited them in. They looked serious and announced that they needed to talk to me. They took turns telling me that I was being rude and unprofessional by reading during rehearsals. They asked me to leave my books at home and be 100 percent there for them while I was on the set.

How dare they prance into my dressing room and tell me what I can and can't do? I'm doing my job, and nobody's complaining—except them. As long as I'm feeding them their cues on time, what's the problem?

I felt my excuses and anger bubble up inside, but only tears flowed out, washing away my chance to be righteously indignant. All I could do was admit that I was wrong and tell them that I was sorry. Once I regained my composure, I thanked them for having the courage to confront me. That's another lesson I have learned from my Father: "To learn, you must love discipline; it is stupid to hate correction" (Proverbs 12:1).

Correction might make me cry, but pruning is "shear" torture. Jesus gives this illustration: "I am the true vine; my Father is the gardener. He cuts off every branch of mine that does not produce fruit. And he trims and cleans every branch that produces fruit so that it will produce even more fruit" (John 15:1–2, NCV). To say that my heavenly Father has been a diligent gardener would be an understatement. There was one time in particular when I thought that He might be Edward Scissorhands in disguise.

It began while we were taping the last season of *The Facts of Life*. As I recall, that was a season of abundant grace in my life. My times with the Lord every morning were fertile. On my daily walks, I was soaking up good Bible teaching by listening to tapes by Joy Dawson, a teacher from Youth With A Mission. On Sunday mornings and evenings and on Wednesday nights, my pastor, Jack Hayford, was feeding me from the Word. I could almost feel my roots going deeper as the Lord tended to all the things that needed to grow in my life.

Then He whipped out the pruning shears.

The first thing to go was the part of the branch that didn't produce fruit, or at least wasn't producing good fruit. This meant cutting off the relationship with the young man I was dating.

Now it was time to prune even the branches that were producing good fruit. I was in the middle of my quiet time one morning when I sensed my Father say to me, *I want you to take everything off your plate, and I will put the things I want back on it.*

I knew instantly what He meant, and I set out to obey Him. I had just registered for another year of acting classes, so I withdrew from them and arranged to get my money back. I took my final singing lesson and didn't schedule any for the future. I had been singing at churches all over the country on the weekends, so I contacted my booking agent and told him not to book any new dates—indefinitely.

I was now free to seek the Lord with all my heart, soul, mind, and strength. What a luxury to spend two hours reading my Bible or an hour singing praise songs! I thought I was ripe for the harvest.

Boy, was I green.

After the pruning came the transplanting. Over the next five years I went from being a single, famous actress, making almost two million dollars a year, to being married, the mother of three, and living in a rented house in the suburbs, making ends meet on a pastor's salary.

The worst part of it is that from the time I was saved when I was ten, I've known that my life was about telling people about Jesus. The Gardener put an end to even that. He made it clear that I was not to accept any more speaking engagements. I rationalized that He would certainly want me to seize every opportunity to tell others about Him, but the few times I tried it, I died on the vine. There was absolutely no fruit. It became clear to me that obedience is more important to God than ministry. I began telling pastors who called,

"Trust me. You don't want me coming to your church because God doesn't come with me." So I stayed home, and although I had three children, I felt barren.

I felt like the bougainvillea plant Steve and I bought last year. It was alive and well and struttin' its stuff while on display, but as soon as we brought it home and transplanted it, it died. Or at least it looked like it was dead. There was no fruit, the leaves withered and fell off, and the twigs were so brittle that they would break if barely brushed against.

Steve and I called the nursery and asked for our money back. They told us to give the plant a little more time to acclimate to its new environment. I'm glad we took their advice. Our bougainvillea is now thriving at home, and so am I.

For me, after so many years of struttin' my stuff for all to see, it was a shock to my system to be brought home. I loved being a wife and mother, but it took a while for me to recognize the fruit because it was a different kind of fruit than I was used to.

Looking back, I can see that the Lord was preparing me for a new season of fruitfulness—in a different garden. He began with minor corrections and proceeded to pruning, cutting away even the good things, until it was time to uproot me, transplant me, and then allow me to bloom where I was newly planted. The resulting fruit was especially sweet.

If there are areas in your life that you know need to be cleaned up, then don't be "stupid" and hate the correction. Learn to love the discipline of the Lord (Proverbs 12:1). If you feel like you are going in a million different directions but producing little fruit, then submit to the "shear" grace of the Gardener. If your life has been turned upside down and your system is in shock, give your roots time to grow deep; there will be fruit again.

The key to a life of fruitfulness is the next thing Jesus says in John 15:5: "Yes, I am the vine; you are the branches. Those who remain in me, and I in them, will produce much fruit." What makes the difference is staying attached to the Vine.

NINE

Circumcision of a Shiksa

For any boys and goys reading this who don't recognize the term *shiksa,* it's a Yiddish word for a non-Jewish girl. And the word *goys* is not a typo, and it doesn't mean a cross-dresser; it's a term for anyone who isn't Jewish.

Thank you, class. That will be all. (See? I knew the Lord could redeem my disobedience in dating that young, non-Christian, Jewish man. I'll talk more about that later.)

I think we're all clear on what the word *circumcision* means. For purposes of clarification, may I tactfully define it as the cutting away of the excess flesh (foreskin) from the male genitalia. In the Old Testament, God told the children of Israel, "The LORD your God will circumcise your hearts...so that you may love him with all your heart and with all your soul, and live" (Deuteronomy 30:6, NIV). The New Testament describes it this way: "When you came to

Christ, you were 'circumcised,' but not by a physical procedure. It was a spiritual procedure—the cutting away of your sinful nature" (Colossians 2:11). Just as pruning back the branches of a plant produces fruit, circumcising the heart gives birth to new life.

You are probably wondering where I'm heading with all of this. Let me tell you about my time under the knife.

Over the years, in addition to picking up a couple of pounds, I had added a little excess flesh around my heart. Nothing too serious—just a little feeding of the carnal nature here, a little indulging in an unhealthy snack there. Nothing to lose my salvation over, but my heart wasn't totally clean—or lean in this case.

The first flab to go was some of the novels I'd been reading. I've already mentioned my voracious appetite for books. Well, I could wolf down a Sidney Sheldon mystery or a Judith Krantz saga in one sitting. Sure they were marbled with fat; that's what made them so juicy.

Then the Lord sharpened the steak knife; it was time to trim the fat. I want to make it clear that the Lord never takes a knife to my heart forcefully. He always waits until I realize that the excess flesh is blocking the flow of His Spirit. Then I willingly submit to the Surgeon's hand. Anyway, I felt my heavenly Father gently impress upon my heart the need to stop reading those kinds of books. I guess He could have suggested that I just skip over the more sizzling chapters, but the temptation might have been too great for a single woman not to take at least a tiny bite.

Now that I'm married, those books don't have the same

danger or appeal. The things that excite a mother are not usually found in a typical bestseller. I really wish someone would write a steamy novel for married women. I imagine it would read something like this:

He laid down the remote and made his way into the kitchen where she was wearily rinsing the dinner plates. As he drew closer, she could feel his hot breath...no, wait, that was just the steam from the dishwater. He approached her from behind, wrapped his arms around her waist, and held her prunelike hands in his. She felt the familiar sensation of moisture as he squeezed the dishrag and water ran down the front of her dress.

He leaned into her body and whispered the words she longed to hear: "Honey, I'll do the dishes for you."

She melted onto the linoleum floor and felt a strange tingle run up her spine. She had inadvertently landed on a Barbie doll.

He reached down, lifted her to her feet, and with a slow, rhythmic motion washed the last dirty dinner plate. She couldn't help herself; her hand reached down and grabbed the large, furry towel in the bottom drawer, and they dried the dishes together until they were mutually spent.

As the man turned to go, he spoke the words every woman aches to hear: "I'll put the kids to bed tonight." That evening something happened that she had only read about, although she had dreamed of experiencing it multiple times—the kids stayed in bed.

Now that's a romance novel for a married woman!

As the Lord continued to encourage me to cut back on my high-fat reading habits, He gave me the option of eliminating Hollywood entertainment/gossip magazines from my diet. I didn't get the impression that they were so bad for my heart, just that they were junk food. There was no need for me to develop such a taste for the world that it spoiled my appetite for the flavor of the things of the Spirit. Besides, you know how it is after you've munched on a bag of potato chips? You've got that greasy residue all over your tongue, and it feels as though your teeth are wearing little socks. That's how I always felt after devouring an entertainment magazine.

I shouldn't have been surprised when the Lord swiftly turned His attention to my choice of movies. This cut was a bit tougher to slice. After all, I argued, this is what I do for a living. I need to include the latest films as a part of my regimen to help me grow as an actress. I was selling, but the Lord wasn't buying.

In the case of movies, I underwent open-heart surgery. The first problem the Doctor detected was a clogged R-tery. It was almost completely blocked from a buildup of R-rated movies. In a similar vein, PG-13 movies had left a surprising amount of plaque deposits. An *f*-word here, a dash of skin there, a romanticized adultery thrown in for spice, a generous serving of violence—heart disease could have slowly snuffed out my life! Maybe that's why they call it the "silent killer."

I'm grateful that the Lord caught it in time.

I can see a big difference in my life now that I'm making more thoughtful choices about what I allow into my heart.

One word of caution: It's important to remember that only the Lord can see into a person's heart. We must be extremely careful not to judge another's choices. What might be harmful for me might be perfectly safe for you. A person who has a history of heart disease in his or her family may have to cut back on fat intake much more dramatically than another person without that genetic makeup.

The same goes for alcohol. I have lots of friends who enjoy an occasional drink and don't have a problem with it. I know other people who realize that they can't handle even one drink. Personally, I have chosen not to drink. In the past I used to enjoy a glass of wine with my husband at a nice restaurant, but one morning, during my devotions, I asked the Lord to fill me to overflowing with His Spirit. I felt Him respond, *There would be more room for My Spirit if you gave up drinking other spirits.*

I had never thought about the fact that another name for alcohol is spirits. I didn't feel any condemnation from the Lord for imbibing occasionally. But when given the choice of having an occasional drink or making more room for the Holy Spirit, it was an easy thing to give up. So, with the exception of special occasions when I have a piece of my mom's triple-chocolate Kahlua cake, I'm a teetotaler.

You may be wondering, *How do you know that it was the Lord talking to you and not your own imagination?* That's a good question. For many years I desperately wanted to hear from the Lord, but I didn't know how to recognize His voice.

Jesus refers to Himself as the Good Shepherd when He says this: "After he has gathered his own flock, he walks ahead of them, and they follow him because they recognize his voice. They won't follow a stranger; they will run from him because they don't recognize his voice" (John 10:4–5).

For me, the key to knowing when God was talking to me was when I realized that I already knew His voice by heart because I was one of His flock. It was the stranger's voice I couldn't recognize.

This played out most dramatically in my early twenties when I began dating the young Jewish man I referred to earlier. He was my singing teacher, and I had a huge crush on him. When I first met him, he already had a girlfriend. During an afternoon singing lesson, I overheard him talking on the phone with her about a concert they were going to that night.

On my way home from my lesson, I called a guy friend of mine and talked him into going to that same concert with me so I could accidentally run into my teacher. My next move was to invite him to one of the tapings of *The Facts of Life.* My schemes must have worked because he eventually asked me out.

But I never intended to fall in love with him. I knew he wasn't a Christian. I was well aware that the Bible says, "Be ye not unequally yoked together with unbelievers" (2 Corinthians 6:14, KJV), which for all intents and purposes can be translated, "Lisa, you know you can't marry your singing teacher, so you shouldn't even be dating him."

I justified going out with him by calling it "missionary dating." That way, as long as I brought him to church with me, there was a chance that he would get saved, and then it wouldn't be an issue.

I knew in my heart that it was wrong. The catch-22 was that as long as we were just having fun together, there was no reason to stay away from him. But by the time I fell in love with him, I *couldn't* stay away from him. He was a kind, funny, talented, good-hearted man who loved me very much and treated me like a princess. That's hard to walk away from. I tried to let go for two years and broke up with him a dozen times. But we always got back together. We were yoked.

We talked about getting married, but every time I imagined myself walking down the aisle, I knew that I would never make it to the *hupa* (Jewish wedding thing). Jesus was right: "They won't follow a stranger; they will run from him because they don't recognize his voice." I recognized that it wasn't the Lord who was whispering, "But you love each other. It's okay to get married. You can still be a Christian, and besides he loves God too." It was the voice of a stranger, so I ran.

But I left a big chunk of my heart behind. If only I had turned around the moment I realized that I wasn't following the Good Shepherd's voice anymore, it might not have been so terribly painful.

Whenever I wonder who is speaking—whether it's God, the devil, or me—I imagine myself following where the voice is telling me to go. If I feel at all uneasy about it, I stop and don't go any farther. If I feel a peace about it, I know that it's safe to follow because it's the familiar voice of my Shepherd.

Do you feel uneasy about any of the voices you are currently following? Stop, turn around, and run from the stranger's voice. It won't be easy, I know. But it will keep you from making a huge mistake.

Has the Good Shepherd spoken to you about circumcising the excess flesh from your heart? Then follow Him, whether the necessary cut is as superficial as trimming a little fat from your entertainment choices or as deep as severing an unhealthy relationship.

"The [stranger's] purpose is to steal and kill and destroy," Jesus says. "My purpose is to give life in all its fullness" (John 10:10). Life and death depend on whose voice you follow.

TEN

The Arranged Marriage

I'm so thankful that I waited to follow the Good Shepherd's voice to find the man I was supposed to marry. I must admit, though, that it didn't happen quite the way I imagined it would. I mean, come on, what daughter wants her Father to choose a husband for her?

Steve and I became friends when I joined a prayer group that he, as a pastor, was appointed to oversee. His boss, Pastor Jack Hayford, had organized "affinity" groups in our church where members who were in the entertainment industry could feel safe being open and transparent about their prayer needs. Our group consisted of four married couples— Michael and Stormie Omartian, Gabri Ferrer and Debbie Boone, Dominic Allen and Charlene Tilton, and Bruce Sudano and Donna Summer. Other than Donna's manager, Susan Munao, and the other pastor, Minnie Whaley, who was an *elder* in every sense of the word, Steve and I were the only single people in the group. Looking back, I can see that it was a Divine setup right from the start.

Our group met once a month, and every month I had the same prayer request. At twenty-two I was ready to get married and start a family, and I wanted to find God's choice of a husband for me. Steve and the others were dutiful to pray. I should have known something was up when Steve asked if he could lay hands on me and pray. Just kidding.

But not entirely…

Over the next two years, Steve and I began to spend a lot of time together, and we became good friends. (Read: I was not attracted to him at all.) Every so often, he would take me out for "the talk"—the one where, because of his integrity and desire not to take advantage of his position as a pastor, he would confess that he was feeling more for me than friendship. I would assure him that although I thought he was a really nice guy (girls, you know what I mean), I was not feeling those same stirrings. We would then resolve to continue going out as friends as long as it didn't get too uncomfortable for either of us.

I had a plum deal. I had someone to go to dinner and the movies with, and my boyfriend wasn't jealous. Oops, did I forget to mention that I had a boyfriend? I'd better fill you in. I had been dating a contemporary Christian singer/musician who was on the road a lot. One weekend when he was home, we were out on a date, and I felt that I had to tell him about my relationship with Steve, just to keep everything up front and—even though he wasn't the Jewish guy—kosher. I mentioned that Steve and I had been spending a lot of time together and told him that because Steve was so "safe," he was the logical person to escort me to functions when my minstrel was out of town. I watched my music man from across the table as he struggled to place the name with a face, "Steve, Steve…. Oh yeah, the church organist! I don't have to worry about *him.*"

So now I had all my little ducks in a row. Well, actually, I wasn't so sure about one little ducky—Steve's feelings. He was so sweet; I just couldn't bear the thought of his feelings getting hurt because of unrequited love. This time I initiated "the talk." As gingerly as possible, I suggested that we not spend as much time together. I encouraged him not to take it personally; after all, I was planning to break up with my boyfriend as well.

I explained that I was going through a personal revival with the Lord. I was even considering joining YWAM (Youth With A Mission) for a mission trip for a year after the last taping of *The Facts of Life.* I told him that it would be best if I just concentrated on my relationship with God for a while. There. I had said it.

I relaxed back in my chair at the same time Steve leaned forward in his. He looked me straight in the eye and declared, "Lisa, I could be good for you."

Where did that come from? Talk about out of the blue. Who had sneaked into the restaurant, kidnapped "Mr. Milquetoast," and replaced him with "Mr. Big"? I was speechless, which is saying a lot. (Actually, it's not really saying anything, is it? Oh, never mind.) I didn't know how to reply, especially since there was something incredibly attractive about what Steve had just done. I decided that it was best not to respond at all, so we ordered dessert and pretended that the entire conversation hadn't happened.

Many weeks passed, Steve and I as friendly as ever, as I continued to wholeheartedly pursue my relationship with God. I registered for a seminar at our church that a visiting evangelist was leading. The last session was to be an anointing service. There were hundreds of people in attendance, and she was praying for them one at a time, so the rest of us waited quietly on the Lord in worship.

I had my hands lifted to the Lord as a gesture of praise when I felt the sensation of a gentle weight descending upon me. I recognized this feeling as the presence of the Holy Spirit. And because this kind of thing doesn't happen every day, or even every year, I knew enough to pay attention. As I waited expectantly, the thought popped into my head, *Would you ever consider marrying Steve Cauble?* I knew that this was God talking because it was the last thing I would ever think of on my own. My knee-jerk response was: *No. Are You kidding?*

I shrugged the Holy Spirit off my shoulders and got back to the business of worship. But the thought would not go away. So I purposed to ponder it in my heart, but I certainly wasn't going to tell Steve about it.

The next day, Steve was leaving town for a week, so after the seminar I visited him at his house. We chatted while he packed; then it was time for me to head home. Just as I turned to leave, he took my hand and led me to the couch. He looked at me with unusual urgency. "Listen," he implored. "Before you leave, I have to ask you one question. Would you ever consider marrying me?"

Wow! This guy doesn't say much, but when he does…it's a doozy. I laughed nervously. "Funny you should mention that," I said. Then I told him what had happened earlier at church, and we agreed that this was something we should pray about. Yeah, I know, pretty discerning, huh?

In my opinion, this called for more than praying—this called for fasting! If you know anything at all about me, you know that something has to be mighty serious for me to think about giving up food. But considering the fact that I had suddenly lost my appetite, it wasn't such a tough decision.

Proverbs 11:14 says that safety comes with a multitude of counselors, so during the following week I met with every pastor or elder I could schedule an appointment with. They all loved Steve and me and thought that marriage was a fabulous idea. But by the time Steve got back from his trip, I was more confused than ever. How could this be God's will? I mean, weren't you supposed to want to kiss the guy you were going to marry? And I really wanted children. How was I going to do *that?*

We concluded that what we really needed was counsel from the Big Kahuna himself, Pastor Jack. He would know what we should do. So Steve called him up, and he invited us to come to his house after the Sunday evening service.

We arrived just as Pastor Jack and Anna's favorite television show, *Murder She Wrote,* was starting. We had to sit there trying to act interested in a show that anyone could figure out within the first five minutes. I wanted to shout, "The butler did it! Now can we get on to something a little less trivial, like the rest of my life?" But I stifled my impatience—thank goodness I'm an actress.

Mercifully, the program ended, and it was time to receive from the hand of the master. We gave a full account of all that had transpired over the past few months. We covered the friendship aspect of our relationship; we addressed the age difference (Steve is thirteen years older than me); we talked about what we thought the Lord might be saying; and we reiterated our desire, above all, to do God's will. The only thing I failed to mention was the tiny detail that I wasn't physically attracted to Steve.

Pastor Jack paused just long enough to break into a broad smile before delivering his blessing. "Sounds good to me." He beamed. "I think you should go for it!" *What? That's it? No alliterated three-point sermon? No big words to look up when I get home?* I was stunned. But before I could react, Anna was offering me a piece of strawberry cheesecake, and we were talking about Jessica Fletcher and that stupid television show again. *Help! I'm on a speeding freight train, and I can't get off.*

Little did I know that this "little engine that couldn't" was about to become a bullet train. Steve left the next day to accompany Pastor Jack to the Foursquare denomination's district conference. After Pastor Jack was introduced, but before he began to preach, a huge grin burst across his face. Steve was like a son to him, and he couldn't wait any longer to act the proud papa. "Before I begin," he said, "I have some happy news to announce. Our very own Steve Cauble is engaged to Lisa Whelchel." Gasps and applause erupted from the crowd.

Let me make sure you have the full picture. Steve knew full well that immediately after the benediction, the Foursquare grapevine would swing into action. It just so happens that Steve's parents are Foursquare pastors too. So he sneaked out of the service and raced to a pay phone to call me. I could tell from his voice that something was wrong. "Uh…Lisa…you might want to get ahold of your mother before someone else informs her of our impending marriage."

"Come again," I said, hoping that we had a really bad connection and that I hadn't actually heard him say that we were engaged. He tried to explain that there had been a little miscommunication: Apparently we hadn't made it clear to Pastor Jack that we had gone to him for his counsel, not his blessing. "Yowser, Bowser!" Steve exclaimed.

I hung up the phone and it hit me: I'm engaged to a man who says, "Yowser, Bowser."

I knew immediately that I would have to leave the church. There was no way I could go through with this. I mean, isn't there a part of the wedding ceremony when the preacher says, "You may kiss the bride"? It might be a bit embarrassing if I offered Steve my cheek. No, I would definitely have to leave the church. There was no way I could continue to attend—every little old lady I passed in the sanctuary would be whispering, "There goes the Jezebel who broke sweet Steve Cauble's heart."

When Steve got back to town, we met for dinner. I anticipated an intense evening of wrestling through our options as we figured out how to clear up this terrible misunderstanding. I was not prepared for how excited Steve was. Did he really believe that because all of Foursquaredom was thrilled about our engagement I was too?

Apparently so, because the next thing he said was: "Well, I guess if we're engaged, I ought to buy you a ring." Why was it so hard for me to say no? Did I really think that I could avoid hurting Steve's feelings forever by continuing this charade? Sooner or later, I was going to have to do the loving thing and break his heart.

I was able to postpone the inevitable for a little longer when he said, "My friend Doug bought Christa an engagement ring at the mall. Let's go look there." Whew, I was off the hook. The truth is that I'd known for a long time what kind of engagement ring I wanted. I also knew—no offense—that I certainly wasn't going to find it at the mall. I was sure that it would have to be designed specifically for me. I mean, really now.

As we drove to the mall, I rested secure in my superior taste in jewelry. The man behind the counter asked me if I had anything in particular in mind. "Well, frankly, I do. But I've never actually seen the ring; I've just imagined it. Perhaps it would help if I drew it." The gentleman handed me a piece of paper, and I proceeded to draw an emerald-cut diamond surrounded by two triangular trillion cuts on each side.

The jeweler studied the slip of paper and then reached into the case and pulled out a ring. "You mean this one?" he asked.

There it was—my ring. The one I had never actually seen

before. *Oh no,* I thought. *I drew it!* I couldn't take it back and say, "Well, no, come to think of it, it was more circular in shape."

Steve was elated. He whipped out his credit card and bought it on the spot. I'm pretty sure I even heard him say, "Praise the Lord." But the Lord obviously had nothing to do with this. I mean, God created man and woman; He created the way they create babies. He knows about these things. Surely He wasn't a part of all these "coincidences."

A few days later I panicked. I caught the first flight to Nashville to visit my childhood friend Michelle. Either she would help me figure out what to do or I could just have my belongings shipped to Tennessee. When I got to Nashville, I went to the local Christian bookstore and bought every book they had on "How to Find the Will of God."

I spent the next three days in bed, alternately poring over these books and pouring out my heart to God. The situation had gotten way out of hand; it had escalated into a crisis of faith. It was more than an issue of whether Steve was the man I was to marry; it was an issue of whether God was the God I was to serve.

The way I saw it, there were only three explanations: This was all a big joke and God had capriciously manipulated our lives for His own sick entertainment; this was all my fault for not having the courage to say no; or this *was* God's plan for my life and I was destined to marry a man for whom I felt very little attraction. To me, all the options were devastating.

I felt that either my past was all a lie or my future was

going to be lived as one—I had to find the truth. What did I know for certain? Let's start at the beginning: Okay, I believe there is a God. I have met Him personally, and He has proven Himself trustworthy in my life many times. I know that I know that He adores me and that He is good through and through. He is stronger than the devil's schemes, and He is more powerful than circumstances, coincidences, or my cowardice. I could rest in this because I also knew for certain that I had sought His will with a pure heart.

The choice was mine. Was I going to trust God or trust my heart? I knew the decision I had to make, and I felt an unexplainable peace about it. When I boarded a plane home, I was wearing my new engagement ring and carrying the "Now That You Are Engaged" book I had purchased earlier in the week. I figured that since I had decided to marry this man whether the feelings were there or not, I could probably use all the help I could get.

The first suggestion in the book was that I title a sheet of paper "What I Love about My Fiancé" and fill it out. I took out a legal pad and began to list all of Steve's wonderful qualities. There had never been any question about how much I admired and respected him, so it was easy. I even recall a time shortly after getting to know Steve when I remarked to a friend, "If the woman who marries Steve Cauble doesn't realize what a prize she has, I will personally pay her a visit and knock some sense into her."

Somewhere around thirty-five thousand feet, before I realized what was happening to me, I had filled not one but two legal-sized sheets of paper with unexaggerated hyperbole extolling the many virtues of Steve Cauble. As I reread my list, something totally unexpected happened.

I fell in love.

When I got off that plane, I ran into my fiancé's arms and gave him the sloppiest kiss you ever did see!

What do you know that you know that you know about God? Do you believe that He is all-powerful? Do you trust that He is all-good? Is He all-loving and all-holy? You need to settle those questions in your heart. There may come a time in your life when the only thing you can count on is the character of God. And it will be enough.

Eleven

Be Still and Know That I Am God

According to traditional wisdom, the first year of marriage is the roughest. For Steve and me, that wasn't true. Our first year was marital bliss. Years two through seven were the killers.

From the moment I walked off that plane and into the arms of my future, everything was a blur. That was February of 1988. The final episode of *The Facts of Life* was filmed in March, and Steve and I were married on July 9.

Our honeymoon was a good indication of how we would spend our first year of married life. We stayed ten days at beautiful Lake Louise in the Canadian Rockies. My favorite memory is of hiking up the mountain during a soft rain and stumbling upon a tiny cabin where they served hot soup and fresh homemade bread.

Steve's least favorite memory is of going on an all-day horseback ride through the glacial mountains (my idea). As a girl I had had my own horse, so I was in heaven. Steve, on the other hand, was not an experienced rider. He took quite a beating when his horse decided to trot most of the way down the mountain. One word of advice, girls: Don't suggest a horseback ride on your honeymoon unless your husband knows how to keep from bouncing in the saddle.

As we were packing up to return home, Steve mentioned that he had always dreamed of going to Hawaii on his honeymoon. This was the first I'd heard of it, so I said, "Let's go." We flew to L.A., where my mother met us at the airport with two suitcases full of summer clothes. We exchanged them for our bags of winter clothes and boarded a plane to Kauai for "Honeymoon: Part Two."

What a privileged life we enjoyed that first year! Steve and I both love to travel, so we took advantage of every opportunity. For my dream trip, we spent ten days in New England enjoying the fall foliage and ferreting out hidden bed-and-breakfasts. For Steve, we made reservations at a Walt Disney World resort and hit as many theme parks and restaurants as we could in a week. It was a yearlong honeymoon.

Ten months into our marriage we discovered that we were pregnant. Surprise! The honeymoon was just about over. It was time to settle down and begin the joyful task of raising a family.

The first thing we did was sell my condo and buy a house with a big backyard. Although I wasn't working at the time, I was still receiving residuals and income from my investments. I assumed that I would get another job and continue working after the baby was born, so we bought a $750,000 house and put an additional $50,000 into it to make it our own.

We proceeded to have three babies within three years—Tucker, Haven, and Clancy. It's hard to get an acting job when you're either pregnant, nursing, in the waiting room at the OB-GYN office—or all three. Needless to say, my days as a working actress were temporarily on hold.

Gone were the days of breezing in to work around nine o'clock, grabbing a bagel from the spread that was laid out for us, and flopping into the makeup chair so someone could "do me over." I was now getting up every morning at five-thirty (or two o'clock, depending on which "getting up" you're referring to). My breakfast was usually whatever was left on the kids' plates before I cleared the table. And I had very little energy left to do myself over.

It's inevitable that at some point early on in your marriage, you will discover that the person you married is not the person you thought you were marrying. Our marriage was no exception. I woke up one morning around year two and couldn't recognize the stranger beside me. (I'm sure Steve felt the same way, but this is my book, so I'm going to tattle on him first.)

Our wedding should have given me a heads up that Steve's personal philosophy is "more is more." Steve is a master of details and class, so he planned the whole wedding from beginning to end. Being a church organist, he had attended hundreds of weddings. I had been to only one, and I was the flower girl in that one.

Steve knew exactly what he wanted: a string quartet, a harpist, seven groomsmen, ten ushers, professional sound and lighting, and a buffet reception to feed a thousand. To this day I run into strangers on the street that say, "I was at your wedding. It was beautiful." And they're right; Steve did an extraordinary job.

But it wasn't without cost—fifty thousand dollars, to be exact. Actually, it *was* without cost. Do you remember in chapter 4 when I talked about the episode involving Natalie that I asked to be written out of? The understanding was that I would not be paid for it since I didn't work that week.

You're not going to believe this. Months later, shortly after the wedding, I received a check for that episode to the tune of fifty-five thousand dollars, enough to pay for the wedding and the honeymoon! So in a very real sense, my Father paid for my wedding.

The extravagant wedding was the first hint that Steve appreciated the finer things in life, but my suspicion was pretty much confirmed when he made the reservations for the Hawaiian leg of our honeymoon. I was shocked to discover that he had purchased first-class tickets and booked the honeymoon suite at the Sheraton Princeville for a week.

I know how to spend money with the best of them, but by nature I'm pretty frugal. I had always flown coach, and I couldn't imagine spending money for two rooms when one was plenty. As you can imagine, money was a source of many arguments in those early years, especially when the economy took a downturn in the early nineties.

During those years, we realized that in order to keep our house we would need to sell off all of my investments. As you may recall, the early nineties was not a very good time to try to unload real estate. We couldn't *give* the property away. But we couldn't keep it either. Our expenses and investment responsibilities totaled over fifty thousand dollars a month. The church where my husband works is very generous, but you can imagine how much of a dent a pastor's salary would make in that amount. And we all know how well mother-hood pays—if we're only talking money, that is.

We held on as long as we could, but the money dried up, and the only thing left to do was get out as fast as we could. We lost everything except our house, and then we lost that too. It was on the market for over a year, and when we could no longer make the payments, we handed it over to the bank for the amount we owed on it and got ready to move out of our three-thousand-square-foot home.

I think you're getting the picture. It wasn't pretty, and it was about to get even more ugly.

All newlyweds have issues that they need to deal with before two separate lives can become one. We got to a point in our marriage when it became obvious that we wouldn't be able to move forward if we didn't first deal with the past. I knew that Steve didn't like change, but I hadn't anticipated his unwillingness to even try. They say that if you're not growing, you're dying. Our marriage was dying.

I was afraid, but I knew I couldn't run. We had three children under the age of three to raise. More important, to leave would have meant denying everything I knew about the Lord and what He expected of me. Our marriage seemed to have come to a standstill, but divorce wasn't an option, so I had to just survive. And that's exactly what the Lord asked me to do—stick with it and survive.

Over and over again during those long, dark years I held on to the one thing the Lord continued to whisper to me: "Be still, and know that I am God" (Psalm 46:10, NIV).

Be still. Given my personality, it was hard to obey. I'm a "do-er" not a "be still-er." It didn't matter. There was nothing I could do but be still.

And know that I am God. He is God whether we recognize it or not. Nothing about that can change—except us. And change me is exactly what He began to do. He started by giving me a gift.

We had given our house back to the bank and had to move. Steve was out of town on business, so it was up to me to find a place for us to live by the end of the month. I bought a paper and spent days looking at homes for lease. Living on one income, most of the houses that we could afford and that were big enough to sleep the five of us were very run-down. I began to despair of ever finding something clean. All my adult life (and most of my childhood), I had been able to afford just about anything I wanted. Now all I wanted were clean floors for my babies to crawl around on and a window over the kitchen sink so I could keep an eye on them in the backyard.

One day, as I walked out of the grocery store, I picked up a *Nickel Ads* paper. In it I came across an ad for a house that was renting for exactly the amount we had determined we could spend. It was less than a mile from where we lived. That afternoon I made an appointment with the realtor, left the kids with my mom, and went to check it out.

When I walked through the front door, I was sure that the lease amount listed in the paper had to have been a misprint. This home had been completely redone. The carpets were brand new, and the kitchen had all new appliances and cabinets. Above the beautiful marble-looking countertop was a huge picture window framing a fuchsia crepe myrtle tree in the backyard.

I wanted this house so badly that I was afraid to even hope that we might qualify to rent it. I knew that it would be next to impossible for the owner of this lovely home to consider our application once he saw our credit information.

That evening I picked up Steve at the airport and took him directly to see the house. He had not seen what else was available in our price range and had nothing to compare it to, so I doubt he fully grasped why I was so overwhelmed. We filled out the application and attached a personal letter of explanation and appeal. The next day we received a call from the realtor informing us that the owner would be willing to meet with us to discuss the possibility of our leasing his house.

He showed up at our house that evening with his girl-friend. When he introduced her—would you believe it?—I realized that I had known her since I was twelve years old. She had been a child-actress, too, and had starred in the serial that Walt Disney Productions had filmed to air on *The New Mickey Mouse Club*.

We signed the lease that night.

When we are still, God sure knows how to be God. That

rental was half the size of the home we had owned, but I loved it more than any other house I'd ever lived in. Losing everything sure has a way of teaching you how to appreciate the tender gifts that come directly from the Lord's hand.

I was already beginning to change, and my heavenly Father was just getting warmed up. The first thing He told me to do was to look for ways throughout the day to thank Steve. This was the complete opposite of what I wanted to do, which was to point out everything he was doing wrong so that he could fix it. Criticizing him in front of other people and soliciting their support for my position strengthened my case that he was a lousy husband and needed to shape up. I was more than willing to show him how he should be doing things.

The Lord was right to tell me to *look* for ways to thank Steve. I had focused for so long on what he wasn't doing right that I could no longer see the good things about him. You know how you're never aware of how many pregnant women there are until you're pregnant and how you never realize how many minivans are on the road until you get one? That's what started to happen. Once I began to notice the little things Steve did that blessed our family, I began seeing signs of his love everywhere.

The next thing the Lord dinged me on was my unrealistic expectations of Steve. From all the books I had read, I was certain that the husband was supposed to lead family devotions every day, support his family financially, keep a budget, clean the kitchen after dinner, put the kids to bed, tell his wife how sexy she looks in her flannel nightgown, and be able to fix anything—unless of course it's during a conversation, at which point he must never try to fix anything. It may surprise you—I know it did me—but Steve didn't measure up.

Isn't it funny how the things you adore most about your fiancé are the things that drive you craziest about your husband? Steve's gift is serving. The Lord has supernaturally anointed him to come alongside Pastor Jack Hayford and facilitate his vision. Before Pastor Jack can think of something he needs, Steve is beside him handing it to him.

The gift of serving is truly a godsend to a dynamic leader. It ain't too bad in a dating relationship either; let me tell you, I certainly enjoyed it. But can you believe that I began to resent this about him after we got married? I was looking for a leader in our home, and I interpreted his servant's heart as passivity. He was turning to me, wanting me to make the decisions and tell him what to do so he could do what he did best, which was to serve. I was hoping to find somebody bigger than me to take care of me by leading.

No matter what Steve did, it was never quite good enough to meet my expectations—until I made them a bit more realistic. Then I discovered that he was more than enough for me just the way God made him.

I was finally ready to knock down the wall that had been built between us. I knew that only one thing was strong enough to crumble it: forgiveness. I not only had to forgive him for the disappointment and the pain, but I also had to cancel his debt and stop making him pay. It was time to release the hurt—and release him. And that's exactly what happened. Once Steve was convinced that I wasn't going anywhere and that I loved him whether he ever changed or not, he was free to risk changing. And he began to do just that.

Have you reached a dead end at some point in your life? A place where there's a brick wall ahead, and you can't turn around and run away? Your only option may be to be still and know that He is God. And in knowing God, you will know forgiveness, mercy, patience, and deliverance. And that's when you will see change in your life, and perhaps in someone else's as well.

TWELVE

Lord, Help Me—Fast

As the Lord continued to change me, He used several unorthodox approaches. The most unusual was a variety of nonfood fasts. Maybe it's because I'm an all-or-nothing kind of gal, but whenever there's an area in my life that needs correction, my Father suggests a fast.

When our financial situation became serious, I had to learn to refrain from buying everything I wanted. This was especially difficult when it came to baby clothes. I could go months, even years, without buying clothes for myself, but I just couldn't resist those adorable outfits for my little ones. It wasn't like they needed more—between baby showers and hand-me-downs they had enough clothes to get them through kindergarten. But those brand-new outfits were just too darn cute for me to pass up.

In order to help me gain some self-control in this area, the Lord put me on a forty-day fast. No matter how precious the outfit or how big the sale, I wasn't to buy any clothes for the kids for forty days. (Isn't it just like the devil to hold a 40-percent-off sale at my favorite children's store as soon as I had taken the pledge?) But the fast worked. One day I would see a dress that Clancy just had to have; a week later I would have forgotten about it completely. And she probably would have outgrown it by then anyway.

That was only the beginning, though—the Lord soon followed up with an even stricter fast. This time, I was to go forty days without buying anything that wasn't an absolute necessity. Before any purchase, I had to ask myself, *Do I really need this, or do I just want it?* We sure did save a lot of money that month!

One thing that helped me in the beginning was to keep a list of all the things I had to deny myself because of the fast. I figured that I could always go back and buy them later. But I guess I wasn't pulling a *fast* one on the Lord, because after a few days I would realize not only that I didn't really need it, but that I didn't even want it that badly.

The lessons I learned about money and myself from these fasts made a big difference in our marriage. For one thing, I had thought that we never had any money at the end of the month because of Steve's spendthrift ways. I had justified my own spending by either buying things on sale or rationalizing that I was buying things for the children, so I wasn't able to see my own lack of self-control in this area. After a forty-day fast, it was easier to think before I bought. (Although I must confess that after the last one I bought the kids matching cowboy and cowgirl outfits to celebrate "break-fast.")

I have been on similar fasts over the years, including a reading fast. Looking for help in my marriage and in my personal trials, I had gotten into the habit of reading Christian self-help books. One day the Lord encouraged me to stop reading those books for forty days and, whenever I would normally reach for a book for recreational reading, reach for my Bible instead.

This was a new concept for me. I had always read the Bible to grow in the Lord, never simply for enjoyment. During my reading fast, I picked up my favorite translation *(The Living Bible)* and discovered the thrill of reading the Bible as a collection of fascinating stories about people and about my Father. And I found more answers in the Bible than in those other books anyway.

One of the answers I found was in Psalm 4. It said, "Don't sin by letting anger gain control over you. Think about it overnight and remain silent. Offer proper sacrifices, and trust in the LORD" (vv. 4–5).

That was another huge step forward in my relationship with Steve. Typically, when I got upset about something, I would let him know about it in no uncertain terms. Then after he left for work, I would call my mother and proceed to tell her all about it. The more I talked about it, the madder I got.

This verse spelled out for me, step by step, how to deal with my anger. When I got mad about something, I told myself that I could really let him have it the next day but that I must be quiet until then. In bed I would voice my grievances to the Lord and then offer praise to Him, trusting that

He was big enough and loving enough to be in control of my life.

Most of the time I was able to leave my complaint at the Lord's feet the next day and let Him take care of it. On those days when I still felt that I had to say something, at least I didn't yell, so Steve was able to hear me better.

As a bonus, Steve and my mom got along better. The grace to fight and then make up is one of the strange and wonderful dynamics of a marriage relationship. It's hard for a mother to hear about her child being hurt by someone and then have Sunday dinner together and pretend like nothing has happened. Pouring out my heart to the Lord turned out to be the best choice all the way around.

My favorite fast of all time was the no-decisions fast. There were a couple of catch-22's in my relationship with Steve. I wanted him to be the leader in our family, but I also wanted to be in control. I resented the fact that he looked to me to make all the decisions, but I didn't like any of the decisions he made.

The Lord's solution to this was to call me to another fast. For forty days I was not to make a single decision. When asked to make one, I had to defer to Steve or to whoever I was with and simply say, "I don't care. What do you think?" For a girl who always has an opinion about what to do and how to do it, this was excruciating—and yet exhilarating.

I first went on this fast eight years ago. Here's what I wrote in my journal then.

December 1993

I feel compelled to go on another nonfood fast. For the month of December, I'm going to try not to make any decisions I don't have to make. Of course, if I'm the only one here with the kids, I'll make whatever decisions are necessary, but if anyone else is involved, I'll ask them their opinion. I seem to feel like my way is always the best way, and why do anything less than the best? I usually get my way just by being a good debater. I'm beginning to see that I use a subtle form of intimidation to maintain control....

Steve has often said that he is afraid of me. I've written that off as a weakness in him without realizing that I just reinforce that weakness with my every breath. I often sabotage what I've been wanting all along—for him to be the leader.

Take this morning, for example. Steve made a calendar for the kids with all of this month's events on it so we can count down the days to each special event. As he was writing down some of the parties, he asked me for the times. In the past (yesterday), I would have said, "There is no need to write down the times. The kids have no concept of time, and they can't read." But today I kept my mouth shut.

Steve loves detail. He loves thoroughness. I, on the other hand, like to keep things in their simplest form. My way is not the *way or even the best way; it's just my way. Had I spoken my opinion, I would not only have robbed the children of the benefits their father's personality can give them, but I would also have subtly eroded Steve's confidence as a father.*

I have wanted Steve to step in and take a more active part in disciplining the kids. If he gets the message that he doesn't know enough about the kids to even create a calendar for them, why in the world would I think he would have the confidence to discipline them?

This month I'm just going to let go. What tragedy will befall us if Steve picks a different picture for the Christmas card than I would pick? So what if white lights outline our house instead of colored ones? What does it matter if he wants to open gifts on Christmas morning instead of Christmas Eve? The kids will not be permanently scarred.

I tend to instantly see how everything could be done better and offer my "help." This month I'm going to see if God can make it without my help.

I was a real stinker, but I began to smell a little bit better after those forty days. I believe that the no-decisions fast has been the most successful one yet. Yes, it changed me dramatically, but the biggest difference was in Steve. In the beginning, it was just as hard for him to make the decisions as it was for me not to. He didn't trust himself, and he was always bracing himself for my "help." Before long, though, he gained confidence in his ability to make good decisions, and I was surprised to discover how wise he is.

Now it has become a habit for me to say, "Whatever you think is best, honey." And I sincerely mean it. These days there's no question about who is the leader in our home. Steve is very aware of my feelings and opinions; he makes sure of that. But ultimately, I trust him to make the final decision. God knew what He was doing when He set up the order of the household. I'm so much happier not having to be in control of everything.

I am deeply in love with my husband. Sure, it took blood, sweat, and tears, but it was more than worth it. The security I feel from resting in Steve's love is one of my Father's sweetest gifts to me.

On our seventh wedding anniversary, as Steve and I began to see the light at the end of the tunnel, I wrote a poem for him noting the similarities between us and the very first married couple. I'd like to share it with you.

Adam and Eve
& Me and You

I am me because of you.
Out of one, God made two.
In the midst of Eden, you were alone.
I was waiting to find a home.
You closed your eyes and my dreams came true.
I found my place beside you.
You gave to me the very part,
hidden within, protecting your heart.
Now I am more than I could be
without you inside of me.
From dust and ashes and a breath from above,
came you and me, an eternal love.
Thank You, Father, for what You've done.
Out of two, You made one.

The fact that I could write a poem like that for Steve is nothing short of a miracle. I remember sitting in a friend's car and noticing a picture of her husband taped inside the sun visor. "I can't imagine ever loving my husband so much that I would want to look at his picture every day," I commented. That was a time when I had lost hope for anything more than survival and staying together for the sake of the children—and my Father.

But these days, whenever I feel that I might succumb to hopelessness in some area of my life, I look at the picture of Steve on my sun visor, and I remember that nothing is impossible with God.

I hope this chapter has encouraged you to believe in miracles. When the disciples were hoping for a miracle but kept coming up empty, they asked the Lord why. He answered them:

> Because of your unbelief; for assuredly, I say to you, if you have faith as a mustard seed, you will say to this mountain, 'Move from here to there,' and it will move; and nothing will be impossible for you. However, this kind does not go out except by prayer and fasting. (Matthew 17:20–21, NKJV)

If you're in the market for a miracle, perhaps you need to consider a fast. The typical food fast (as opposed to fast food) is another way of telling the Lord that He is the only thing you need to sustain you. When we deny our flesh, which tells us we must have food in order to live, we are truly depending on the Lord for our strength.

Is there something in your life that you are becoming a bit too dependent upon? What are you looking to, other than the Lord, for fulfillment, security, or hope? Can you give it up for forty days to give the Lord a chance to do a miracle?

THIRTEEN

Behind Closed Doors

Much of my life has been a series of deaths and resurrections. That's okay. In fact, Jesus said that that's the way life should be: "I tell you the truth, unless a kernel of wheat falls to the ground and dies, it remains only a single seed. But if it dies, it produces many seeds" (John 12:24, NIV). Some kernels, however, die harder than others. My acting career was one of the hardest seeds for me to plant in the soil and then walk away from and let die.

It never crossed my mind that I would not continue to work after the birth of my first baby. I was going to be a mother of the nineties. I had grandiose plans of hiring a nanny, turning my dressing room into a nursery, and bringing Tucker to the set with me. I just assumed that I would get another job. But with the exception of one feature film that went straight to video, I never got another job I auditioned for. I guess I needed to learn my lesson about assuming anything!

Nevertheless, it took me a while to get the message that God was no longer blessing my career. Every time that kernel of wheat fell into the soil to die, I dug it out again and went for another audition. I just couldn't imagine that I wasn't supposed to continue in show business. Why would God bring me this far just to leave me? Didn't He want me to be light in a dark place? He certainly had to know that if I didn't work, we would lose our home and everything else. It just didn't make sense. Maybe that's why the door was not simply closed, but slammed in my face. Otherwise, I might still be knocking.

The nameplate on the door read Aaron Spelling. I had worked for him several times over the years, and he had always encouraged and supported me. His office called my agent and personally requested that I audition for his latest television series, which was about a husband and wife team who were actually angels in disguise. He was aware of my Christian beliefs and thought that this would be a perfect part for me. I, too, thought it was meant to be. For one thing, the show was going to be filmed in Texas. I saw this as my ticket back home.

I walked into the audition and sensed right away that every person in the room was ready to give me the part. From my first professional audition at the age of ten—when I won the title role of Heidi in a summer play—until I was cast as Blair at sixteen, I got almost every job I auditioned for. I was used to winning. All I had to do was give a halfway decent reading, and the part was mine.

After all the niceties and kissy-kissies, I launched into the scene. About two lines into the dialogue I could tell that something was wrong. As hard as I tried, I couldn't connect. I began to panic. I felt like a skater must feel when she's in the middle of her program and has already fallen on her first two jumps. She knows that she has to finish the routine, but it doesn't matter, because she has already lost the competition. I wanted to stop in the middle of the scene and skate off the ice crying.

Mercifully, Mr. Spelling himself stopped me. He gave me a new direction to try and offered me another chance. I gave it my best shot, but it was no use. It was gone, and I couldn't get it back. I was so awful that as I left nobody even offered me the standard Hollywood "good reading" line.

I sat in my minivan feeling sick in the pit of my stomach. I was so embarrassed that I had given such a terrible reading. I could understand if it wasn't God's will for me to get the part; what I couldn't understand was why I had to be so humiliated in the process. There was no way to convince myself that "they chose to go another direction" or "the director's girlfriend got the part." I had blown it, plain and simple. I tried to praise the Lord. I knew in my heart that my life was in His hands and that one lousy reading couldn't change the course of my life unless He allowed it.

Shortly after that my agent dropped me from his roster of clients. By then I had Tucker and Haven and was pregnant with Clancy. I was beginning to get the picture that the Lord wanted me to stay home and be a full-time wife and mother.

Still, it didn't make sense financially or practically.

I wasn't willing to let that kernel die, at least not completely. So I had another one of my brilliant ideas! I could be a voice-over actress. That way I could stay home with my children, make some money occasionally, and still do something creative with my life. Wrong again. It was the same story: Everyone wanted to hire me, but I wasn't good enough. If there was ever a doubt in my mind that God had graciously opened the door to success in my career and that it had nothing to do with my talent, He made it perfectly clear when it was time to close that same door.

Eventually, my manager retired and moved to New Jersey. I made no attempt to find another one; after all, God had always been my primary agent, and He had stopped representing me years ago. I was finally ready to accept the death of my acting career. Once I realized that for this period of my life God's hand of blessing was reserved for my home, I was able to rest.

Well, maybe *rest* isn't the best word. I think you'll understand why if you take a look at an excerpt of an article I wrote for our church newsletter during that season of my life.

FIVE MINUTES OF PEACE

Today is my husband, Steve's, day off. He has just walked out the door to go to the car wash with our three-year-old son, Tucker, and our eighteen-month-old daughter, Haven. Now, with our four-month-old daughter, Clancy, asleep in the closet (there are only so many rooms to go around), I have five minutes of peace. How should I spend these next precious minutes?

The thrill of it is too much for me to handle. Compulsively, I cut out the coupons from Sunday's paper. Why did I do that? Now I only have four minutes left. I mustn't squander this treasure of time.

I could take a nice, hot, Mr. Bubbles bath. But then again, look at this kitchen! It looks like a Cheerios box exploded sometime when my back was turned. No, this time is for me. What should I do? The Lord would probably appreciate hearing from me. I mean, something other than *Please let them all take a nap at the same time today.* Maybe I should get on the treadmill and try to make a dent in this last ten pounds of baby fat.... Naah!

Oh no! Did I hear what I think I heard? It came from over there, near the baby monitor. There it is again. It can't be. She can't be waking up already. I still have three more minutes of peace left! I'll run and put the pacifier in her mouth.

Whew! It worked. But I really must make a decision about these last three minutes. I sure could use a nap. ....*Hmmm.* Last night we got home from church too late for baths. So after pj's, pottying, and prayers, the miracle occurred—quiet! I fell into bed, already halfway to REM sleep. I leaned over to kiss my husband good night only to come face-to-face with that stupid grin. *Here's my chance,* I thought. I adopted that same stupid grin while casually remarking, "In the morning, I sure would love to sleep in." He bought it! He agreed to get up with them. We were both happy…. I'm still tired, but would I really feel rested after two minutes of sleep? Probably not.

I've got it. I'll brew a cup of hot tea and read the new book my mom got me for my birthday three years ago. "Once upon a time…" Uh-oh! There's that sound again. The pacifier must have fallen out. I guess that answers my question about my last minute of peace.

When I wrote that article, I could still remember when my most difficult decision was where to go out for dinner. What a difference five years, one wedding, and three C-sections had made! One night when an actress friend of mine said, "It must be nice to take a break after working for so many years," I was tempted to slap her with a wet wipe. I'd never worked so hard in my whole life.

For three years I felt like all I did was pick up toys, coordinate naps, and kiss boo-boos. But I began to realize that there was a whole other level to my life and that I'd never had a more important job: I was teaching my children how to respond to God.

When I taught Tucker to obey me the first time without arguing, it was more than my need to maintain some semblance of control. In those crucial first few years, he was establishing patterns that will be with him throughout his life. If, years from now, God gently says, *No, she is not the girl I have for you to marry,* maybe he won't come back with, *But*

I love her. You don't understand, and choose less than God's best for his life.

When I waited to give Clancy her bottle until it had been close to three hours since her last one, it wasn't because I was rigid about a schedule. It was so her tiny body and mind could learn patience, security, and delayed gratification early on. God has a plan for her life, and she can trust Him to fill her with just what she needs in His perfect timing.

When Haven was just starting to talk, one of her first words was *please.* I taught my children to say *please; thank you; yes, ma'am;* and *no, sir*—not just because I'm from the South and it's good manners, but because I wanted to spare them a lot of pain by instilling in them a respect for authority. There will come a day when they'll face a choice between doing what's right and doing what everything in them cries out for. Perhaps the deciding factor will be what the Word of God says and the respect for its authority they learned while they were young.

Being a full-time mom is the hardest job I've ever had, but it's also the best job I've ever had. The pay is lousy, but the rewards are eternal. I will be forever grateful for the privilege of being a stay-at-home mom. The cost was dying to myself and my career, and that was scary. But the scarier thing is that I could have missed it.

I suppose it's human nature to fear death. The unknown is frightening. The good news is that as Christians we know what happens after we die, so we don't need to be afraid of physical death. The same is true of life. We know what happens when we are willing to lay down our lives and die to our plans.

Jesus Himself showed us. Had He not been willing to lay down His life and die, we would not have been able to receive life. And unless we are willing to lay down areas of our own lives and let them die, we may never experience the abundant life He has planned for us.

FOURTEEN

Hand It Over

"Daddy, tell us about when we were in Mommy's tummy."

Thus began a seemingly innocent conversation in the car while we made our weekly pilgrimage to Costco, the warehouse store where you can buy five of everything you need in handy five-gallon sizes.

Seeing that Tucker was strapped beyond arm's reach in his booster seat, Haven taunted her brother. "Tucker, you can't have a baby 'cause you're a boy. Only girls can have babies!"

Not to be one-upped, Tucker shot back: "Yeah? Well, get ready, Haven, 'cause they're going to get a knife and cut your belly open to get it out!"

Trying to head off toddler trauma, Steve intervened. "Not necessarily. Not all babies have to be cut out."

I shot Steve a quick "Oh no, don't go there!" look, but it was too late.

"Then how do they get out?" came Clancy's tiny voice.

Realizing that he had passed the point of no return, Steve tried to sound nonchalant. "They come out of Mommy's private area."

"Eeeww, yuck!" the kids chorused.

"I sure am glad I didn't come out that way!" Tucker said.

Tucker might have been relieved that he hadn't come out the yucky way, but I wasn't. I was very disappointed when my doctor told me during my thirty-ninth week that my baby was upside down and that if he didn't turn around in the next forty-eight hours, I would have to have a C-section.

I couldn't believe it! We had just finished Lamaze classes, and I had broken the hospital record in the sniff-sniff, shee-shee, hold ten, long-blow event. I was ready to go for the gold! But as it turned out, I didn't even qualify for the finals.

From the moment the little stick turned blue, indicating my second pregnancy, I was determined to have this baby "like a real woman." I had many conversations with my doctor, and he assured me that I would be able to have a VBAC this time. I was relieved, thinking that that meant lying on my back with my legs in the *V* position, which is what I had wanted the first time. Then he told me that VBAC stood for "vaginal birth after cesarean." Even better!

As soon as my water broke, my contractions started coming fast and furious. By the time we got to the hospital I was ready for the epidural. I asked the parking attendant to give it to me, but he wouldn't. After checking in to my room, I changed into something a little more comfortable—my hospital lingerie with the easy-open back. The nurse untied the little string, and I finally felt the pain to end all pain, the blessed epidural. I was home free! I had made it through the hardest part! My doctor arrived, and I assumed my regular conversational pose while he checked my progress. He assured me that everything was going fine and that I would be able to push any time now.

I relaxed and went back to watching the *Tonight Show,* and he left to fill out his reports. A few minutes later he came back and began checking my digital hookups. Suddenly, he said something to the attending nurse, and she went scurrying out. Then he told me that the baby's heartbeat was erratically dangerous and that he was going to have to perform an emergency C-section.

I was crushed. My dream was not to come true. I couldn't believe that I had made it through the hardest part and still wasn't going to experience a traditional childbirth. As they were wheeling me down to the OR, I heard the Lord whisper to me, *Rejoice in all things.* Through clenched teeth, I muttered, "Okay, Lord, thank You that I'm having this C-section. I will praise You in all things, and I will rejoice in You."

I saw the look on the doctor's face when he made the incision. There was a gaping hole just beneath the first layer of skin. My previous C-section scar had ruptured six of the seven sewn layers, exposing a small window. In an instant I realized that if I had delivered my daughter Haven the way I had wanted to, we would not have known about the rupture until after much internal bleeding and possible oxygen-deprivation for the baby.[1]

And that's not even the big miracle in this story.

Haven was born with an often-fatal blood disease called Group-B Strep.[2] The mother harbors this disease in the birth canal, and the baby ingests it as she passes through during delivery. But my baby never passed through the birth canal. If she had, she surely would have died. Even after her case was reviewed by the hospital board, it's still a mystery how she contracted this disease. But it's no mystery why she survived. And again I say, "Rejoice." Sometimes the Lord says no to our dreams in order to birth something healthier in our lives.

That was just the first time that the Lord intervened and miraculously saved Haven's life. The second time was a year and a half later when she was staying at my mother's house. She was playing with a drawerful of dishrags in the kitchen one minute, and the next minute she had disappeared.

Discovering that she was missing, my mother peered out the back window at the swimming pool, but she couldn't see it because it was a long way from the house and screened by a tall hedge. Then she walked into the living room and noticed that the back sliding glass door had been left open. She ran toward the pool, and as soon as she passed the hedge, she caught a glimpse of the top of Haven's head at the end of the pool.

It was wintertime, so the pool was covered by two pieces of plastic that ran the length of the pool and overlapped about a foot in the middle. Apparently, Haven had crawled out onto the plastic. Waist deep in water and crying, she was sitting on top of the plastic in the middle of the deep end of the pool.

There were two miracles here. The first was that she made

it out onto the plastic without slipping into the water, because the edge of the plastic did not meet the pool's edge— it missed the wall by at least six inches. The second was how she kept from slipping between the two pieces of plastic in the middle where she was sitting.

My mother dove under the first piece of plastic, swam underneath, and came up through the middle. She caught Haven's wrist just as she was going under and lifted her up above the water long enough to smoosh down the plastic and drag Haven behind her as she swam to the edge of the pool. She was not strong enough to stay afloat and lift Haven out of the pool at the same time—and that was when miracle number three occurred. My nephew Chasin just *happened* to come outside at that moment. He saw his grandmother struggling and came to her rescue, lifting Haven out of her arms so she could pull herself to safety.

Tucker also has miraculously escaped death twice. Once when he was a baby, he was sitting in the seat of a shopping cart with a giant jar of pickles beside him. (Don't ask why we needed a giant jar of pickles—we were at Costco again.) Outside, the shopping cart hit a crack in the pavement and toppled over. The only thing between Tucker and the concrete was the glass jar. If you could have seen the large shards of glass sticking up, you would have deduced, as we did, that it was a miracle that Tucker walked away (if he could have walked) with only a few minor cuts.

When he was a little older, he and I were almost run over by a car. We were in the driveway of my mother's house, and it was dark. I had buckled Haven into her car seat and walked around to the other side of the minivan to strap Tucker into his. I set him down beside me just long enough to lift up the car seat bar and brush out the cookie crumbs. I reached down to pick him up, but he was gone. He was running full speed toward the five-lane boulevard at the end of the driveway.

My mother was already running after him, but I passed her. She later said that it was obvious I had been infused with the Supermom adrenaline that kicks in when your child is in danger. Without looking, I lunged into the first lane of traffic, grabbed Tucker, and, clutching him to my side, stared straight into the headlights of an oncoming car. I don't know how I was able to pull us both back to safety before the car zoomed past, but I'm pretty sure it involved the help of an angel.

Why am I telling you all these stories? Well, for one thing, I have learned through these experiences that I must trust my heavenly Father to keep what is most precious to me. There will be many times in my children's lives when I won't be able to ensure their safety. And as they get older, especially during their teenage years, the task will be even more difficult than just protecting them from physical harm.

A few weeks ago at a Thursday evening prayer meeting, I became particularly anxious about some of the attitudes I see developing in my children as they approach puberty. Although my husband and I have done our best to instill godly principles in them, I was beginning to realize that the quality of their lives ultimately depends on the choices they make in their hearts. I desperately want to protect them from making mistakes that could cost them the abundant life that

God has planned for them, but as I sat there I began to realize that I have very little control over something that means so much to me.

As the prayer meeting was winding down, our pastor said, "If there is anyone here who desires prayer for an issue we haven't covered tonight, please stand." I immediately got to my feet. I felt like Jacob did after he wrestled with the Lord: "I will not let you go unless you bless me" (Genesis 32:26).

As I stood, the Lord met me. He did not answer my prayer, but He did bless me. My prayer was that the Lord would cleanse the ugly areas festering in my children's hearts. Instead, the Lord whispered a Scripture to this mother's heavy heart: *I know the one in whom I trust, and I am sure that he is able to safely guard all that I have given him until the day of his return* (2 Timothy 1:12, TLB). My Father knew that what I really needed was to again surrender my children into the hands of the One who is able to keep them for eternity.

What are you holding on to for dear life? A dream? A relationship? Security for the future? Hand it over to the Lord. He can be trusted to take care of that which is most important to you. He may not handle it the way you would, but you can believe that whatever the outcome, you will be able to rejoice in all things. On the other hand—or better yet, *in* the other hand—if your dreams call for a miracle, they're in the right place.

1. You can find more information regarding Uterine Rupture on the Internet at www.groups.yahoo.com/group/unterinerupture.
2. You can find more information regarding Group-B Strep at www.groupbstrep.org.

FIFTEEN

Daddy's Little Girl

Clancy has experienced her fair share of God's miraculous hand. Let's begin with conception. (I guess we all begin with conception, huh?) Clancy's may not have been a miracle, but it was definitely one of those "God things." You moms reading this will be able to appreciate the magnitude of this little beginning.

Let's see if you can get the picture. I have a toddler who just turned two and keeps me running all day, a new baby I'm nursing who keeps me up all night, and I'm recovering from a C-section that had complications. Then, "Surprise!" There's only one word for Clancy's conception—immaculate.

I suspected that she was in there, but knowing that conception would have been this side of a miracle, I didn't mention it to Steve. There was no need to get him all worried if I was just running a little behind schedule. So one Monday morning on the way to the local IHOP for a Rooty Tooty

Fresh 'N Fruity, I asked Steve to stop at the drugstore so I could pick up something. I bought an at-home pregnancy test because I couldn't find any at-restaurant pregnancy tests, and that's where I was planning to take it.

The hostess led us to our favorite table, and after setting up the high chair and the infant seat, picking up several crayons, opening a package of crackers, and propping up a bottle with a burp rag, I ran to the bathroom. I mean it: I ran. Do you remember back in the olden days when you had to take a pregnancy test with the first *sample* of the day? Needless to say, there was a certain urgency.

As I waited in the stall, I watched the little plus sign appear. I was positively thrilled. I came running out of the bathroom holding the happy stick! Steve's initial response, however, was not as enthusiastic. Okay, let me be blunt: It was years before he could eat another pancake without getting that sinking feeling in the pit of his stomach.

Toward the end of my third trimester, I began feeling sharp pains in my lower abdomen. I was also going in and out of premature labor. My doctor prescribed Tributaline and put me on bed rest. This is a rather cruel combination. Although the drug suppresses the contractions, it makes your heart and everything else race—but you are sentenced to bed.

Somehow "Son, I'm on medication to prevent premature labor, and I must remain here on the couch all day while you play quietly in your room" didn't cut it. Thankfully, Haven wasn't yet mobile, so I only had to get up every three hours to feed her, every two hours to change her, every thirty minutes to pick up her pacifier off the floor, and every fifteen minutes to restart the baby swing. So much for bed rest.

We set the C-section date for Clancy to be born on my stepfather, Roy's, birthday. We were very glad that she waited long enough to arrive on his big day. Although I didn't go through an extended labor, that little window of my previous scar that had ruptured during Haven's birth had already torn apart again. Who knows how long I had been walking around with a womb with a view?

Clancy passed her Apgar test with flying colors and advanced to her first bath. Then Daddy was allowed to hold and rock her in the hospital nursery while Mommy was being stitched back together. My mother was watching adoringly through the window when Steve suddenly jumped up from the rocking chair and handed Clancy to the nurse. Immediately, a half-dozen additional nurses ran into the room. Wrappers went flying and needles began poking. Then a nurse saw my mother. She pulled down the shade and ushered Steve out. He explained to my mother that he had been holding and rocking Clancy when she just stopped breathing and began turning blue.

The doctors and nurses revived Clancy and sent her to the neonatal intensive care unit for further testing and observation. The first set of X rays showed a small hole in her lung; hours later, the second set was clear. In between the two X rays, during a Wednesday evening prayer service, our entire church prayed. It's pretty clear to me what happened.

Nonetheless, for ten days she stayed in the neonatal nursery on antibiotics around the clock. The morning of the day we were finally allowed to take her home, we met with our pediatrician and a pediatric cardiologist. Our doctor said that she had heard some irregularities in Clancy's heart during an earlier exam and wanted to get the cardiologist's opinion.

As he examined our baby, we could tell that something was wrong. Removing the stethoscope from around his neck, he told us that Clancy had been born with a small hole in her heart. He assured us that this was not life threatening but that it could mean open-heart surgery. He encouraged us to take our baby home, not to worry, and to make an appointment to see him in a couple of weeks.

At that appointment a couple of weeks later, we learned that in babies born with an atrial septal defect (ASD) the hole sometimes grows together on its own without surgery. The doctor told us that babies recover much faster from the surgery than older children do. He recommended that we schedule surgery right away, but he also said that he understood if we wanted to wait a while. We definitely wanted to wait. We knew that God had knit Clancy together in my womb and that He could certainly complete the job on His own.

Over the next two years, the hole in Clancy's heart did not close at all, and the doctor told us that there was now very little hope of it ever closing on its own. He suggested that we go ahead and schedule the surgery before she got much older. Steve and I have always been grateful for doctors and for healing that comes through medical science, but for some reason neither of us felt that we were supposed to schedule the surgery yet. We assumed that this meant the Lord was planning to heal her supernaturally.

For years, a loving signs-and-wonders-believing church,

multiple itinerant healing evangelists, faith-filled grandparents, and trusting parents prayed for Clancy. The hole remained the same. Each year we had the same discussion with the doctor: He recommended surgery; we were not opposed but didn't feel the release to schedule it. So we continued to believe for a miracle.

When Clancy turned six, we knew that it was time to do something. One night, after she had hopped out of the bathtub and was drying off, I noticed a bulge beneath her chest— the effect of a heart muscle that had to work extra hard to compensate for the leaking blood.

So many questions! If God hadn't planned to heal Clancy supernaturally, why had He led us to wait and hope for so many years? And besides, why didn't He just heal her in the first place? What about all the hundreds of prayers? Confused, but at peace, we scheduled the surgery.

Open-heart surgery would mean putting Clancy on a heart-and-lung machine while her own heart was stopped. The surgeons would then make an incision from the top of her collarbone, down the front of her chest, to the bottom of her rib cage. They would have to break her breastbone in order to reach her heart and sew up the hole. She would then need weeks to recover from the broken bone and the large incision. The scar would be there for life.

It was hard for me to accept that my little girl had to go through such a violent operation when I knew that God could point His finger toward earth and heal her in an instant. I didn't understand, but I knew that I could trust my Father.

We proceeded with the necessary preparations and met with the cardiac surgeon. Unbeknownst to us, great strides had been made in repairing hearts with ASD in the years since Clancy was first diagnosed. The surgeon to whom we had been referred was a pioneer of a new technique that enabled surgeons to repair the hole without the need for broken bones or foot-long scars.

The surgeon told us that in just the past year he had begun performing the operation by entering through a small incision under the right breast. He would then go under the breastbone and repair the hole. As Clancy developed, her breasts would cover the small scar, and there would be no visible indication of the surgery.

As I listened to the surgeon, I was suddenly struck by the intimate concern of a heavenly Father who cares so much about how a young girl might feel about her body that He had us wait to schedule her surgery until the perfect time. I think God knew that the message we sometimes need to hear today is not what a great and mighty God we serve— although He is that—but rather what a tender, loving Father we have, even when He says no.

I don't know why God didn't answer the multitude of prayers for this sweet little girl, but I do believe that the same powerful, wise, and loving Father who tells me no is the same one who tells me yes. I can trust Him even when I can't understand Him.

But it's not always easy. I'm struggling even now with disappointment and confusion because I want more children but haven't been able to conceive for nine years. Can you believe that I had three children three years in a row and, although nothing has changed, I can't get pregnant again? I have questions, but they don't contradict my conviction that God gives us the desires of our hearts. God knows that my ultimate desire is for His will—in His way and in His time. And if He says no, I will say thank you.

Are you feeling barren where there was once life? Is there a hole in your heart that you wish God would reach down and supernaturally heal? Let me encourage you to continue to wait with faith. God may not perform a miracle, but He is trustworthy to touch you and make you whole where there used to be a hole.

SIXTEEN

Home Sweet Home

Many people ask me why I decided to homeschool my kids. I wish I had a more impressive answer. It's kind of like how I feel when people ask me how I got saved. I'm tempted to explain, "Oh, I was sitting in the corner of my jail cell, coming down off some heavy drugs, when the Lord intervened, and from that day forward I was not the same ten-year-old." That sounds like a much more dramatic testimony than "I was led to Christ by some hot, fresh doughnuts."

The truth is that I stumbled into homeschooling. When Tucker turned four, I called my Aunt Polly, who had been a public school teacher for years, and asked her what I could do to help prepare him for kindergarten. He hadn't attended preschool, and although I was certain that he knew how to hold scissors properly, color within the lines, and write his name backward and forward (we were working on correcting the backward part), I wanted to make sure I hadn't failed to address any of the finer points of kindergarten curriculum.

Aunt Polly encouraged me to invest in a good phonics program to give him a head start on learning to read and an early math workbook to introduce him to addition and subtraction. Tucker and I spent about an hour every day "playing school" while the girls took their morning naps.

When the time came to enroll Tucker in kindergarten, he was ready for first grade. I knew that I didn't want to make that leap, so, because kindergarten is not mandatory in California, I kept him home for another year. I bought him a few more math workbooks and easy readers and also began teaching phonics to Haven. Clancy joined us in her high chair for arts and crafts time. I mentioned earlier that as a teenager I was homeschooled before homeschooling was cool. Well, as an adult, I was homeschooling before I knew I was homeschooling.

After Tucker turned six, I had to make a decision about his schooling in the fall. Even though I have an aunt, two cousins, and a couple of good friends who are fabulous public school teachers, I was nervous about enrolling our kids in the local elementary school. The alternative, private school tuition times three, was not a possibility on a pastor's salary. So for the first time I seriously considered homeschooling as an option.

The more I investigated, the more excited I became. What had seemed like a last resort was turning into a first-rate preference. Following my MO, I immersed myself in research. I scoured the Internet, bought volumes of resource books, attended conventions, subscribed to two magazines, and sat in on local homeschool "covering groups." I had been completely unaware that there was an entire underground network of curricula, support, and resources available.

At my first homeschool convention I spent the first couple of days attending lectures. I left each class feeling more and more confident that I really was capable of teaching my own children. I met wonderful women who assured me that I wouldn't have to do it alone. New support groups were springing up every day to provide everything from organized sports programs to high school science labs to tea talks for stressed-out moms.

The last day of the convention I walked the exhibit hall. Wow! Every kind of curricula imaginable was available. There were textbooks for the independent learner, video courses for the visual learner, unit studies for the kinesthetic learner. If I'd looked closely enough, I probably could have found a course of study specifically designed for the redheaded, left-handed, right-brained learner who enjoys studying under a tree and standing on his head while drawing pictures.

The next question for me was: "What about the problem of socialization?" But when I assessed Tucker's schedule, I quickly realized that the only socialization problem was how I was going to limit his socialization enough for him get any schoolwork done. He had church choir on Wednesday nights and baseball practice on Thursday afternoons. Friday mornings were my Good Medicine Club game group for moms and play group for the kids. He had ball games on Saturdays and Sunday school the next day, and then Mondays were

Daddy's days off. Throw in playing with the neighborhood kids on Tuesdays, and it was obvious that Tucker was not going to become a maladjusted social misfit.

I have thoroughly enjoyed homeschooling my kids. Sure, there were days when I would have loved to send them off to school so I could do something fun—like go to the grocery store by myself. But there's only a brief window of time when I can pour my heart and soul, and ultimately God's ways, into my children all day long. That's my primary focus as a homeschooling mom.

Homeschooling has given me the opportunity to really put Deuteronomy 6:5–7 into practice. It says, "Love the LORD your God with all your heart, soul, and strength. Memorize his laws and tell them to your children over and over again. Talk about them all the time, whether you're at home or walking along the road or going to bed at night, or getting up in the morning" (CEV).

When my children were younger, I was able to instill in them the kind of behavior that the Lord says will bring blessing to their lives. Often when I corrected them, I told them specifically what God's Word has to say about their choices. That's so much more effective than offering "Because I'm the mom and I say so!" as an explanation. And because I was with them all day, it was easier to make progress without having to undo what they had picked up outside the home.

As my children get older, I'm finding it beneficial to be around them as they begin to develop attitudes that are displeasing to the Lord—and to me. These heart issues are subtle, and I'm thankful that the kids are near me throughout the day so I can help nip bad attitudes in the bud before they develop into full-blown adolescent rebellion.

That's what homeschooling is all about for me: bringing God into everyday life lessons and helping my children grow in Him intellectually, spiritually, and practically. The fact that Tucker, Haven, and Clancy are getting a thorough, solid education with no chance of falling through cracks in the system is just a bonus.

If you decide to homeschool, it may be more appropriate for one season of life than another. I can speak from personal experience here. After homeschooling each of my children from the beginning, last year I enrolled all three of them in a Christian school. The previous year I had attempted to write a book and homeschool them at the same time, and it was a disaster. I figured that I had better get them into a different educational environment before I attempted to write another book so they wouldn't end up back at holding scissors properly, coloring within the lines, and writing their names backward. Thankfully, they were ahead of grade-level at the beginning of the year, because by the end of the year they were right on target.

A more traditional school situation has been a valuable experience for both the kids and me. I've learned the art of making lunches with only a can of tuna and some tortillas. I'm much more diligent when it comes to checking pockets and backpacks for important papers, wads of money, and yesterday's leftovers. I've gathered a plethora of ideas for breakfasts that can be eaten in the van, and I'm becoming proficient in the art of negotiating carpooling and play date exchanges.

The kids have learned that handwriting is graded, that we live too far away for me to bring their homework if they forget it, and that book reports are less stressful if you don't wait to write them until the night before they're due. They have also been introduced to playground politics, the pain of cliques, and that *gay* means something other than *merry*. These are all important life lessons, and it was a year of good growth for our entire family.

This year the kids are again being homeschooled—or motor-homeschooled, to be precise. We're taking our classroom on the road for a yearlong adventure across America. We'll be living in an RV and stopping to visit historical sites, factory tours, and national parks while promoting my books. Ahh…the beauty of homeschooling.

I understand that homeschooling might not be the right choice for every family. I love it; some moms would hate it. I feel that I'm cut out for it; some moms would rather run barefoot across broken glass. My children seem to flourish with one-on-one teaching; other children depend on competition and the pursuit of good grades to spur them on to excellence.

One thing I do know is that the Bible doesn't have a commandment saying that one way is right and the other way is wrong. I believe that we should be very careful not to impose our personal beliefs and preferences on others regarding differences of opinion that are not spelled out in Scripture. Paul wrote, "Don't criticize [the Lord's followers] for having beliefs that are different from yours. What right do you have to criticize someone else's servants? Only their Lord can decide if they are doing right, and the Lord will make sure that they do right" (Romans 14:1, 4, CEV).

I think that's sound advice for many situations. If you are struggling to make some difficult decisions right now that aren't specifically addressed in the Bible, don't make a choice based on what's right for someone else. You are the Lord's, and He will make sure you do what's right.

Seventeen

A.D.H.D. Is
H.E.L.L.

At the age of six, Tucker was diagnosed with ADHD (Attention Deficit Hyperactivity Disorder) by two different doctors. As his mother, I don't think that's what he has, but the symptoms are the same, so I still deserve the sympathy. Perhaps a portion from my book *Creative Correction* will explain what I mean.

From the moment of conception, I started reading parenting books. Well, okay, maybe not right at that particular moment, but soon thereafter. I determined that if there was a right way to raise children, I was going to find it. Steve and I attended our first parenting classes before we even took our Lamaze classes. We certainly didn't want to ruin our child for life by neglecting a crucial ingredient in the first few months of infancy. We found out later that we had already blown it by not reading Plato aloud and playing classical music while he was in utero.

After Tucker was born, I continued to read books on every subject from colic to college. We also attended classes on high chair manners and hosted water-baby swimming lessons. By the time Haven and Clancy showed up, Steve and I were parenting experts.

Life was rolling merrily along until the arrival of El Niño. (For those of you who don't remember, El Niño was a warm front that brought massive rain to the West Coast.) Suddenly, Tucker became irritable, hyperactive, and often uncontrollable. He had been somewhat moody in the past, but we had chalked up his erratic behavior to fatigue and crankiness. With the onset of El Niño, however, Tucker started to wake up that way.

We assumed that we were not being strict enough, so we buckled down more tightly. But our discipline would only send him screaming to his room, kicking toys along the way and slamming the door behind him. Even more confusing, the very next day he would wake up and be the enjoyable and affectionate little boy we had grown to know and love. It was like living with Dr. Jekyll and Mr. Hyde. We explored every possible explanation, visiting over a half-dozen specialists. Tucker went through fifteen bottles of vitamins, nine months of allergy shots, six homeopathic remedies, five elders who prayed for healing, three weeks of elimination diets, two Hepa filters for air purification, and one light box for Seasonal Affective Disorder. The majority of the doctors diagnosed him with ADHD and recommended medication.

But there was one glaring inconsistency. He was an absolute angel during the summer months. This had nothing to do with school, either. Noticing this pattern earlier, we had already begun homeschooling him throughout the summer and taking a break during the winter when Tucker's ability to focus was next to nil. This approach had been relatively successful.

It wasn't until the next year, after El Niño had come and gone—leaving our family as if it had been hit by a tornado as opposed to a deluge of showers—that we realized the common thread: weather changes. Apparently, when the Santa Ana winds, a cold front, or rain sets in, Tucker's allergies go haywire and so does his behavior. Unfortunately, they have yet to make a rainy-day pill.

The year of El Niño was by far the roughest, but in all honesty, nine months out of every year we feel as though we've been hit by a storm. Tucker is a great kid. He's hysterically funny; he loves the Lord sincerely; he has a bucket of charisma and a ton of friends. I have no doubt that he will be very successful in life, no matter which paths he chooses to explore.

Having said that, let me also say that raising Tucker has taught me more about stepping outside of the box, being nonjudgmental and longsuffering, controlling my anger, throwing myself on the Lord, and listening to that still, small voice than anything else I've done in my life.

Let's begin with stepping outside of the box. Homeschooling has been a godsend for us. The flexibility alone has saved us untold amounts of grief. There are days when it's a stretch to expect to accomplish anything more than getting through the day without climbing back into bed and pulling the covers over my head. On those days, I kiss the VCR and the mouse and live from educational video to software program until Daddy comes home.

On a more productive day, I'm still free to mix up the school day to compensate for Tucker's excitement for the exciting and boredom with the boring. His routine changes a lot, but it usually looks something like this:

- Solve twenty-five math problems.
- Shoot twenty-five hoops.
- Practice one page of cursive.
- Feed the dog.
- Trace spelling words in the box of colored sand.
- Jump on the trampoline for fifteen minutes.
- Read a chapter of a biography.
- Eat a piece of fruit.
- Edit a grammar page.
- Write an e-mail to Grandmother.

By nature I'm a list lover. I would much rather give Tucker a list of school assignments, send him to his desk, and tell him that he can't leave his room until he's completed everything. My instincts tell me that this breeds perseverance, self-motivation, and good study habits. But my experience tells me that it fosters arguing, threatening, and lots of tears. I've learned not to rely totally on my instincts.

If I didn't have the luxury of homeschooling, I wouldn't be opposed to having Tucker take medication. I understand that there are many valid arguments on both sides of the debate, and I weighed them all thoroughly before I enrolled Tucker in a traditional school last year. I decided that if at any point during the school year the advantages of not taking medication were overshadowed by the benefits of a healthy self-image, I would choose to have him take the medication.

I can tell Tucker all day long that he's a good kid and that I love him just the way God created him, but if he's getting into trouble all day long and making bad grades because he's unable to conform to a classroom setting, his self-esteem could take a beating. At that point, I would thank God for modern medicine, pray against any unknown, long-term effects, and do my best to make school the best childhood experience possible.

Raising Tucker has also cured me of any temptation to judge other people's children or parenting skills. I know first-hand what it's like to do all the right things and get all the wrong responses. I also know what it's like to do all the wrong things for the right reasons.

I have yelled until my throat hurts. Why? **Because he won't listen if I talk in a normal tone of voice!** How else can I get him to stop talking long enough to hear what I'm saying? One of the biggest breakthroughs in our family life came when I realized that yelling doesn't work. I knew that it wasn't right all along, but I was willing to try it anyway if there was a chance that it might get through to him.

I was ready to give it up only when it became clear to me that, first, yelling to get him to listen to me only made him yell back at me so he could argue louder. Then I had to discipline him for yelling at me in addition to whatever I was correcting him for in the first place. Second, no one could win when we were both so caught up in the moment that our emotions were running the show. As the intensity heated up, the whole situation took a nosedive. Only after we both calmed down did we stand a chance of actually communicating. I should have just trusted what God said: "The anger of man does not achieve the righteousness of God" (James 1:20, NASB).

I have learned not to have a conversation unless we can both speak in a self-controlled tone of voice. When Tucker disobeys, it helps to send him to sit on his bed while I retreat to my bedroom or finish whatever task I'm in the middle of. If I'm tempted to indulge my frustration by raising my voice, this affords me the opportunity to cool down and say a quick prayer for help before I enter into a discussion with him.

If Tucker begins by raising his voice or being disrespectful, I can calmly inform him that he must go back to his bed until he can continue the conversation with more respect and less high-octane emotion. There have been evenings when he has fallen asleep before he could master enough self-control to talk it out. One wonderful surprise has been that after he's had a chance to calm down, Tucker makes the right choices with a good attitude the majority of the time.

As is typical with the Lord, much good has resulted from the challenges our family has faced with Tucker. I guess the most obvious would be the birth of my first book, *Creative Correction.* Traditional child-rearing methods didn't always work with Tucker. In fact, they often made things worse. So I had to get creative.

In situations where I initially might have resorted to the top-three methods of discipline—yelling, time-out, and spanking—I was forced to ask the Lord for help. Out of desperation, I began to sigh a prayer every time Tucker needed to be corrected: *Dear Lord, what should I do?* The question was almost rhetorical, but the Lord would take me literally and drop an idea into my mind and inspire me to try a unique kind of discipline. Much to my surprise, it worked!

Eventually I got the picture that my heavenly Father was willing to help me raise my children and that He is a very creative God. I have begun to listen for and trust that still, small voice when I have no idea what to do. That's not to say that I'm not still holding out for the day when Tucker finally outgrows this "stage." But until then, I'll continue to throw myself on the Lord when it's too much for me to handle on my own.

Knowing that God is faithful to complete the good work He has started in Tucker (see Philippians 1:6), I'll trust Him when the reality hits me that I can't control Tucker and that sometimes he is truly unable to control himself. The answer for both of us is total dependence on our heavenly Father. I'll endure hard days, tired days, rowdy days, and failure days with patience. Thankfully, it's not entirely up to me. God is Tucker's heavenly Father too.

I love the Scripture that says, "He comforts us in all our troubles so that we can comfort others" (2 Corinthians 1:4). It's my hope that the struggles I'm facing as a mother will somehow encourage you. It's funny how I am often more comforted when I find another mom as frazzled as I am than when I run into an apparent Supermom. (I use the word *apparent* because there is not a parent that is a true Supermom; it is merely an apparition.)

Depending on the stage of life you're in, you may or may not be able to relate to my story. But I bet there is some challenge in your life today that produces a comparable sense of frustration, despair, or fear. May I encourage you to turn your attention first to the Lord and then to others? Ask God if He has a creative way to help you in the middle of your trial. And then look around and see if there is someone else you can help. You have a perspective to offer someone in a similar situation that is much more convincing than anything I could say to her. Why? Because I haven't walked in her shoes. But you have, and you have the opportunity to come alongside her and say, as I now say to you "Let's walk together."

EIGHTEEN

Nothing Matters

A couple of years ago an agent friend, Susan Munao, called me one evening and asked if I had ever considered writing a book. I told her that the thought had crossed my mind but not strongly enough to pursue it. I was at a point in my life where I felt much more comfortable walking through doors the Lord was opening rather than pounding on closed ones to get a response.

Susan said that the reason she was asking was because she was going to meet with a publisher the next morning for breakfast to discuss a book deal for one of her clients. He had asked if she knew of others that might have a book in them, and she had thought of me.

I realized that this could be a "God thing." I had visited this particular publisher's booth the previous summer at the Christian Booksellers Association (my husband was there to help our pastor, so I had tagged along), and Susan's call was enough of a *coincidence* to get me to the breakfast meeting. I didn't want to write a book just to be writing a book, but I told the Lord that if He had a message for me to convey, I was willing. To make a long story short, the meeting began a chain of events that eventually led me to write *Creative Correction*.

If I had known what writing books would cost my family and me, I would never have shown up for the coffee and Danish. I had spent the previous ten years as a full-time wife and mother. I will forever treasure the peace and joy I experienced living that simple, singularly focused life. It will never be the same again.

I was given ten weeks to write my first book. Up until that point the extent of my writing experience had been our annual Christmas letter. I felt as if I'd been walking around the edge of a swimming pool, thinking how refreshing the water looked, and then suddenly gotten thrown into the deep end. I didn't want to write a book! I wanted to *read* a book while lounging in the sun. Or, at the very most, play around in the kiddie pool with my kids.

Now I had signed a contract to write a book, and there was no chance of getting my old life back. Sure, I could have called up the publisher and said, "I've made a terrible mistake. I just want to be a wife and mother, and nothing is worth giving up this season with my family." But I knew deep in my heart that that would have been walking away from the Lord's will.

There is no question that God orchestrated every detail that led up to that moment. I wrestled with Him then, and I continue to wrestle with Him to this day over the timing of all of this writing business. Why couldn't He have waited until my kids were grown before He called me to work?

I think I know the answer to that question, but I still don't understand it. I remember talking with a pastor friend several years ago. I confessed to him that I couldn't figure out what was the purpose of *The Facts of Life* thing. Since I was a little girl, I've been aware that I've had a call on my life to tell other people about Jesus. But although my experience on *The Facts of Life* was extremely enjoyable, I couldn't see that it had much eternal significance.

While I was writing *Creative Correction,* it dawned on me. The very girls who grew up watching the show and who counted me as one of their friends are the same young women who have little children today. Because I was "there for them" as they navigated through their own childhoods, it was more likely that I would be allowed to speak to their lives when I offered ideas for raising their own children.

That revelation was comforting on two levels: It helped me believe that I could make more of a lasting impact on someone's life than just providing a few chuckles every Wednesday night. And it gave me a reason to believe that giving up my own desire to just be a full-time mom could ultimately make a difference in a young mother's life and, subsequently, in the lives of her children.

Although believing that has given me something to hold on to, we as a family still had to go through a grieving process. My writing has been the reason for many tears for Tucker, Haven, and Clancy. Because I am unable to write at home where there are so many distractions, I have had to go away for days at a time.

The children have enjoyed many aspects of attending a traditional school, but I have sat on the edge of each of their beds on different nights as they pleaded with me to let them be homeschooled again.

I've never been a very good cook or housekeeper, and now I'm even worse. We are sick of eating fast food, walking across a crunchy kitchen floor, and looking through the dirty clothes hamper for something to wear.

I hope this doesn't sound like a pity party. I thank God every day for the privilege of being used by Him. I also hope this doesn't sound overly dramatic. It's just that letting go of something I cherish as much as the time I spend with my children has been like a death. Not that I wouldn't gladly die for the Lord, but death is still painful. I don't think there is anything wrong with not wanting to die, as long as we're willing to do it anyway.

Thankfully we've been given a beautiful promise of the Lord's presence during times of death. You know this one: "Yea, though I walk through the valley of the shadow of death, I will fear no evil, for thou art with me" (Psalm 23:4, KJV). This promise came alive to me through an encounter I had with the Lord in the middle of writing *Creative Correction.*

Steve had to go to Dallas on business, so I made arrangements for the kids to stay with their grandmother so I could go with him. He would be working all day, so I brought my laptop in anticipation of getting some work done in the quiet hotel room while he was gone.

That afternoon I sat staring at the blank screen of my computer for what felt like an hour. I was trying to write a second draft of my first submitted chapter, which had been returned along with a page of notes from the editor. What was I doing trying to act like a writer? I cried aloud, "I want to give up!" I don't think I had ever spoken those words before in my whole life.

Dear God, I prayed, *You created the heavens and the earth out of nothing, and You are going to have to do the same thing with this book because I have nothing to offer.* I sat back in the chair and cried some more.

Then this Scripture came to my mind: "I lift up my eyes to the hills—where does my help come from?" (Psalm 121:1, NIV). I couldn't remember the rest of the verse, so I searched for it using my Logos Bible software. I couldn't believe what the rest of the verse said: "It will come from the Lord, who created the heavens and the earth." God heard me, and He promised to help me! I almost burst into tears again, this time for joy and relief. God created matter out of nothing. Once I realized that I had nothing to offer, God was ready to create something that really did matter.

When I arrived home the next day, a letter was waiting for me on the table. It was from a friend in Maryland that I hadn't heard from in more than five years. I opened the letter and read, "Lisa, I was spending time meditating on the Lord, and He brought you to my mind. I don't know exactly what this means, but He impressed upon my heart to write you a letter and tell you this: 'Don't give up.'"

If that didn't convince me that my heavenly Father was actively involved in the intimate details of my life, then nothing would. King David understood this when he wrote, "O LORD, you have examined my heart and know everything about me. You know when I sit down or stand up. You know my every thought when far away. How precious are your thoughts about me, O God! They are innumerable!" (Psalm 139:1–2, 17).

So I didn't give up. My heavenly Father stayed right beside me all the way, encouraging me and assuring me that He had called me to begin writing this book and that He would be faithful to enable me to finish it.

As we endeavor to walk in Jesus' footsteps, making sacrifices and dying to ourselves shouldn't surprise us. Don't run from those times—embrace them. You will always gain more by losing, and by dying you will experience abundant life. I have witnessed this phenomenon in my own life, even with regard to my writing. Any time I gave up with my children has already been returned as we travel the country together as a family promoting the book. Take my word for it, you can't lose when you choose to lose.

Better yet, take God's Word for it. Jesus said, "I assure you that everyone who has given up house or brothers or sisters or mother or father or children or property, for my sake and for the Good News, will receive now in return, a hundred times over, houses, brothers, sisters, mothers, children, and property—with persecutions. And in the world to come they will have eternal life" (Mark 10:29–30).

NINETEEN

Father, Give Me Ears to Hear

Okay, I lied in the last chapter. I write more than just our annual Christmas letter. I keep a journal and write in it whenever the kids say something funny, I'm feeling melancholy, or I have an encounter with the Lord that I don't want to forget.

I have a terrible long-term memory. I don't know why. I probably knew at one time and then forgot. I could blame it on the aspartame in too many Diet Cokes. Then again, I've heard that a bit of a woman's brain leaves along with the placenta each time she gives birth. I'd blame it on genetics except for the fact that my nanny is eighty-eight years old and has the memory of an elephant. I don't know what causes it, but I do know this about myself: I have to write it down or I'll forget it.

Other than a few fond memories of isolated camping trips here and there and a handful of "something I did bad when I was a little girl" stories, I remember very little about my childhood. Sadly, I don't remember much about my children's childhoods, either. That's why I'm thankful I discovered scrapbooking when my kids were small. Since then, I've taken tons of pictures and not only of special events. I know myself better than that. If I don't document everything, I won't be able to remember any stories to tell my grandchildren.

I have to admit that I've been known to take my self-assigned role as our family's photohistorian to extremes. Two Christmases ago, Steve fell off of the roof while taking down the icicle lights. Unable to move, he lay flat on his back on the driveway at the foot of the ladder. I was away at an all-day scrapbooking party, and Haven was outside helping her daddy. She immediately ran into the house and called her grandmother, who dialed 911.

Clancy reached me on my cell phone, and I rushed home. I was only minutes away, but I made it home in seconds, arriving before the ambulance but after the paramedics. When I pulled in the driveway, they were cutting off Steve's shirt and pant legs. He was conscious, and if you don't count two broken arms and one broken leg, he was just fine.

When I tell you what I did next, please cut me some slack. I went into the house and got my camera. I took pictures of the paramedics checking Steve's vital signs, strapping him onto the board, and putting him into the ambulance.

A look of horror mingling with the tears in her eyes, Clancy looked up at me and said, "Mommy, how could you take pictures at a time like this?"

"Honey," I explained, "this is an important event in our family's life. We are going to want to remember this."

"I don't ever want to think about this day again!" she assured me.

The paramedic taking care of Steve understood. He took one look at me clicking away and said, "Scrapbooker?"

I took pictures throughout the entire ordeal. I have snapshots of the emergency room, the X rays, and the hospital room full of flowers. I caught Steve in his wheelchair, his walker, and his storm trooper leg brace. I snapped him going into surgery, working with his physical therapist, and sitting, discreetly covered, on his shower stool. Five months later I took pictures of him returning to work.

Then I developed all the pictures, put them in an eight-page scrapbook spread, and wrote down the whole story of how the Lord miraculously saved Steve's life and protected him every step of the way. It's a written reminder of the Lord moving in the life of our family and will be a testimony to our children and grandchildren and great-grandchildren. (I use all archive-safe materials so, theoretically, the scrapbooks should be around for the great³-grandchildren, even if I'm not.)

Obviously, we won't be able to photograph some of our encounters with the Lord. But we can write them down, not only to remind ourselves of those times, but also as a witness to the generations of family to follow.

When Abraham first entered Canaan, the Lord met him and said, "I am going to give this land to your offspring" (Genesis 12:7). To commemorate the Lord's visit, Abraham built an altar. In my journal, there's a section I call "Altars." It's reserved for stories I want to remember forever—stories about times when I know I have encountered the Lord. Here's an excerpt from an altar I built (wrote) a few months ago. I'd love to share it with you.

The most wonderful thing happened to me today, and I just have to write it down. Let me start at the beginning.

About six weeks ago, someone alerted me by e-mail that Walt Disney Productions had placed some of the mouseketeer ears from *The New Mickey Mouse Club* up for auction on eBay. I was very disappointed to discover that my ears, the light pink ones, were not among them.

A couple of weeks later, I received another e-mail reporting that my pink ears were up for bid. I was so excited! For years I'd wished that I'd had the forethought to ask Disney for a pair of my ears when the show was canceled. Here was my chance to acquire them and pass them on to my children and grandchildren.

Most of the ears auctioned the previous week had gone for around two hundred dollars. I was willing to go as high as five hundred, even though my mother had told me that no amount of money was too much to pay for my ears. "They were a part of your childhood," she said, "and you will want to pass them down to your children."

I marked the final day of the auction on my calendar, and that night I put the kids to bed early so I could be on-line for the last thirty minutes of the auction and make sure that I wasn't outbid. As a sat down at the computer, a still, small voice whispered to me from Matthew 6:19–21: "Do not lay up for yourselves treasures on earth, where moth and rust destroy and where thieves break in and steal; but lay up for yourselves treasures in heaven.... For where your treasure is, there your heart will be also" (NKJV).

You see, I'd been reading a book by Randy Alcorn entitled *Money, Possessions, and Eternity* because I was searching for God's perspective on whether to invest money or give it away. The book had already convinced me that when we give money away, we are actually investing it—in heaven. Giving money away is the perfect investment: It's risk free and the return is astronomical.

Now the Lord was calling me to live out what I had learned. *Oh, but, God,* I argued, *You certainly don't want me to pass up this once-in-a-lifetime opportunity to own my ears, do You?* But as I thought about it, I realized that five hundred dollars had the potential to change someone's life. Somehow my desire to own a piece of my childhood paled in comparison.

I felt a peace about bidding up to two hundred twenty-five dollars, just in case I wasn't really hearing from God. *If God does want me to have them,* I reasoned, *it will be an easy thing for Him to let me win for twenty-five dollars more than what some of the other ears went for.*

Well, I wasn't on-line more than ten minutes before the bidding passed my cutoff point. Although I had to struggle with all my might not to place a higher bid, God had spoken, and He had said no. I watched as the bids rose over even my five-hundred-dollar mark. The ears eventually sold for over six hundred dollars. I was very disappointed, but I knew in my heart that I had obeyed.

The next day I sent an e-mail to the gentleman who had bought the ears. "Congratulations on winning the pink ears," I wrote. "Those are the ears I wore on the show. If you ever decide to sell them, would you please give me the opportunity to try to purchase them? Thank you." (This was just in case God changed His mind.)

I received a reply from James Comisar, who, as it turns out, owns a company that collects TV memorabilia. He very graciously informed me that he would have paid far more than he did for the ears because he was going to put them in his museum alongside my *Facts of Life* Eastland uniform, which, by the way, he already had. He told me that I was welcome to bring my children to visit my ears any time I wanted to.

Until four days ago I thought the issue was settled. Then I received another e-mail from him. He said that he had a gift for me and that he'd like to meet me at the Saugus Café. I thought perhaps he had another piece of memorabilia from the show, or even maybe one of the other sets of ears he had purchased in the earlier auction for two hundred dollars.

Well, I met him today, and after a very nice lunch, he presented me with the pink ears! To say that I was shocked would be an understatement. Little did I know, this was only part of the surprise. He then went on to tell me the story of how he had come to the decision to give me my ears.

Earlier in the week, after two days of hard work preserving and restoring the ears, he was ready to archive them in one of his climate-controlled warehouses until the next time he wanted to display them. He arrived at the warehouse, popped in a CD of TV theme songs, and began unloading his truck. As he was carrying my ears from the truck to the shelves, these words popped into his head: *I wonder if these belong with Lisa's family.*

Realizing that this was not something he would normally be inclined to consider, and though he is not a particularly religious man, he reasoned, *Well, if this is something I'm supposed to do, I need a sign.* Before the last word was formulated in his mind, the warehouse speakers rang out, "You take the good, you take the bad, you take them both, and there you have *The Facts of Life*...." He knew at that moment that something (or Someone) bigger was happening.

As excited as I am about owning my mouseketeer

ears—and I am thrilled—I'm even more blown away by the touch of my adoring Father's hand reaching down to give His daughter a gift beyond what she ever would have asked or imagined. I'm recording this in my journal as an "altar" to remind me of the intimate relationship God desires to have with His children.

We think that we will never forget times like this when we meet the Lord, but I have found that time has a way of stealing the most valuable things, even from people that have better memories than I do. When I say "meet the Lord" and "valuable things," I'm not talking about supernatural, audible-voice kinds of encounters or material possessions. God meets us every day with His riches.

Build an altar when the Lord breaks through in your marriage or heals your child or answers a prayer. Build one when you understand a certain Scripture for the first time or when you're so overwhelmed with gratefulness that you just have to get it down on paper. Leave a heritage for the next generation that will stand forever as a testimony to God's faithfulness in meeting our needs—and meeting us.

TWENTY

Love, Mom

My mother has left a heritage to me through her letters. In this way, and in so many other ways, she is my role model. For Mother's Day a few years ago I gave her a framed quote by Abraham Lincoln that reads, "All that I am, or hope to be, I owe to my mother." That is how I feel. With the obvious exception of my heavenly Father, my mother has had the greatest influence on me, from the inside out.

I say from the inside because so much of who I am today I simply inherited from my mother. As any daughter can attest, it's eerie when you wake up and realize you're becoming your mother. Thankfully, for me that's a good thing.

My mother has spent a lifetime teaching me how to be a parent, mostly by example. She was 100 percent involved in my life. She was my Girl Scout leader, my softball coach, my

Sunday school teacher, the room mother in my class, and the president of the PTA.

She not only made my clothes, but she also sewed matching outfits for the two of us—and coordinating clothes for my Barbie doll! When I went away to summer camp, I got mail from her every day. I always received a box of cookies on the very first day. She had to have put them in the mail before she even put me on the bus.

My mother convinced me that I was the most beautiful, talented, intelligent, perfect daughter who ever walked the face of the earth. (No one can tell me that hearing that all their lives won't make a difference in children!) But just in case her message wasn't coming through loud and clear, she wrote me letters. At many of life's turning points, my mom sat down and put her love, encouragement, advice, and vote of confidence on paper in black and white.

Will you indulge me and let me share some of her letters? You'll have to keep a few things in mind. She is very prejudiced: In her opinion, I was the most beautiful baby ever born and the most perfect daughter who ever lived.

You'll immediately recognize from whom I inherited my writing style. Her humor is just a wee bit weird. That said, you'll know to take some of her "advice" to me with a grain of salt.

The first letter is one she wrote to me right after I graduated from kindergarten. I was already grown the first time I read it, but it seems that no matter how old you get, there's still a five-year-old inside that could use a hug from Mommy. This letter is a hug in cursive.

❦

June 1, 1969

My Dearest Daughter,

This year has closed with many happy memories for you, and, of course, watching you has been my loving memory. As this year of kindergarten began, I watched you go so eager and full of life, always willing to try new things and join in.

I always wished I could take your picture every morning as you hopped out of the car—so fresh and beautiful. I can close my eyes and see you as you turn to wave a final good-bye.

As the year progressed, you became more independent of me and demanded more of yourself. You begun to learn so much, so fast. You have always been so smart and quick to learn.

When graduation day came, I wanted you to get your hair cut, but you always wanted it long. So after much hassle, we did not cut it. I fixed your hair up on your head in curls, and we had to put a jar of Dippity Do on it to make it stay up in the back.

I wanted you to have a new dress so badly, but the money was unavailable. I shouldn't have worried; you looked like an angel in your pink dress.

My darling Lisa...you looked so beautiful and so grown up. You were the prettiest thing I have ever seen. It seemed like God had taken the most beautiful flowers in heaven and colored your face. It just shined.

I felt like my heart would burst when you walked up to say your name, address, and phone number. You adjusted the microphone just like a pro and spoke so clearly. After we got home, Daddy said, "Without a doubt, Lisa was the best one."

Darling, this year has been a good year for you. But in a way it has been a sad year for me. I see how much you have grown up and how fast the year has gone. Oh, how fast time flies. I wish I could go back and really enjoy you without worrying about spoiling you.

Lisa, I want to tell you how much I love you. You are the sunshine of my life. I know that you will grow more precious to me every day of your life, but I wanted to tell you how much I loved you when you were five.

I love you so—

Mother

P.S. God has given you to me to mold and guide until you are grown. Darling, I hope I can do the kind of job that you will be proud of when you are grown.

You did, Mom, and I'm proud of you. So much of how we see ourselves as adults is the result of the picture our parents painted of us with their words when we were children.

My mom wrote this next letter during those critical self-image-shaping teenage years. She had joined me on a French Riviera cruise while I was filming a *Love Boat* special. As I recall, I was discouraged because I had a crush on one of the actors, who wouldn't give me the time of day. He was dating a bombshell, and I felt fat, ugly, and rejected.

Dear Daughter,

Rockin' and rollin' over the ocean and thinking about how happy you have made me on this trip. Seeing you as a woman for the first time. I'm so proud of you, darling. You are so strong and good.

I wish I had never let you get involved in this acting stuff so you would be off at some nice college getting ready to marry some nice Texan. It hurts only being with you a few days a month.

Lisa, never, never settle for less than the best—in anything or anybody. You are the best and therefore capable of obtaining the best. (Plus, you will be bored in time if you don't.)

You don't have to compete. You already are what every woman wants to become. You were born with a specialness that cannot be attained through artificial substance or coyness. You have depth and plenty of it. Hold out for the things you want. Don't compro— Oh, I know you won't; you never have.

Remember how special you are, exercise from time to time, (every other season), and wear high heels occasionally, and you'll be okay.

Love,

Mom

P.S. Where are you and what are you doing while I'm writing at this time of night?

My favorite letter is the one my mom wrote to me to give me some advice about finding a husband. To put it in context, you need to know that my mother didn't approve of the young man I was dating. She didn't think he was good enough for me. (Of course, she had picked out John F. Kennedy Jr. for me at birth. How could anyone compete with that?)

As you read, remember what I told you about my mother's prejudice and weird sense of humor.

August 6, 1986

Dearest Lisa—

My very best friend in all the world! I pray for you a wonderful husband and companion in life.

Pick the right one, sis! Every man who has a relationship with you will fall in love with you—you can't help that—don't feel guilty about this. God made you that way. Don't worry about the hurt they will feel when you are gone—knowing that you will have so enriched their lives that the pain will manifest itself as growth.

You are special; make sure you marry someone special. I don't mean that in a haughty way. I just mean that a lifetime is a long time to live with someone. It can be wonderful if that person is many-dimensional (and not merely demented).

But what if you make a mistake—the old "love is blind" theory, where you don't notice the wart on his nose until after the honeymoon? What if you ask, "Hey, how are you doing?" and he says, "I don't want to talk about it!"?

What if you never noticed that he never has any new ideas or doesn't want to go camping with the kids? What if he said, "I love children and I want a dozen of them, but I never said I was going to help with them"?

What if the same guy you used to have long philosophical conversations with only wants to spend his time in his workshop in the basement building birdhouses because that's what his daddy did—and you live in a condo and don't have any place to put a birdhouse?

There's only one way to prevent the above and avoid waking up in the middle of the night in the middle of the second year screaming, "I MESSED UP!" Check him out! Not once or twice, but seventy times seven.

- *Get to know him over a long period of time. What's a couple of years when you are thinking about a fifty-year relationship?*
- *Check out how he treats his friends, but mostly how he treats his enemies. What's the worst he has to offer? Don't wait until after the knot tying to find out. Tick him off on purpose—not just once or twice, make him mad several times.*
- *Look his family over. Does his father have a wart on his nose? Does his mother spend inordinate amounts of time in the workshop building cookbooks?*
- *How do his coworkers feel about him? Disguise yourself as a piece of office equipment one day and just*

hang out and listen and watch. See if he puts his quarter in the "honor jar" for coffee when no one is around.

- *What kind of student was he? Look up that third-grade teacher and get her side of the story about the missing Christmas tree ornament.*
- *How about the child in him? What really happened those first three years of life? Interview his preschool teacher for early signs of dullness.*
- *And last and most important—MONEY. If he has it, adjust to his irritating habits and just stay gone a lot.*

Love, Mom

When I was pregnant with my first child, my mother wrote me two letters. The first was a beautiful card full of equally beautiful words. The second was actually two little homemade books, which she had filled with practical pregnancy and parenting tips.

11/89

Lisa—

God's Word tells us that the gift of a child is a blessing, but I also believe this must be a very, very special baby for God to have blessed it with a mother like you.

You will be so wonderful, darling. You were born to be a mother. You have plenty of "good mothering" in your genes through Nanny and Grandmother. That, combined with the Spirit of Jesus in you—well, you just can't beat the natural and *the supernatural, can you?*

I've never been prouder of you than I am in this time in your life. You are fixin' to play the most difficult role to date and the most rewarding. You are so capable, so ready.

Love,
Mommy

THE PAIN AND GAIN OF PREGNANCY AND PARENTING

- As soon as the stick turns blue, begin eating anything you want and remember to get two trays at cafeterias.
- In order sleep in, extend the morning sickness thing into the seventh month.
- Now, about labor—whine and complain about everything.
- Feign sleep when they bring the baby in. You'll have plenty of time for holding him when you get home. That bonding stuff is overrated.
- Tell your husband that your doctor said that due to complications, absolutely no conjugal visits for three months after birth.

Now here are some tips for raising kids:

- Don't change a diaper until the baby's too heavy to pick up.
- Leave dirty diapers in the kitchen garbage cans of disagreeable relatives.

- Let them sleep in their day clothes; it cuts down on laundry.
- Take the kids to Grandma's every Friday night, and pick them up on Sunday night. You deserve to have two days off. Alternate grandparents if one set starts to look sick or weakly.
- Be sure to tell them to tell their grandparents how they don't have the things the other kids have. Have them pack a couple of broken toys—nothing obvious, just an arm or a wheel missing.
- Teach them to develop their individuality. Have them wash with a towel and dry off with a washcloth.
- Express your own individuality. Wear your gown all day, but dress for bed.
- Meals—now, just don't get that started. Provide plenty of finger foods like cookies, chips, and small candies within easy reach. They like these things, and it eliminates the hassle vegetables create.
- Volunteer for room mother, insist on being chairman, and then let everybody else do the work.
- Prepare them for the future—name them after rich relatives.
- Encourage your kids to make friends with only children. They always have to cart playmates to their homes, and sometimes they will get invited on vacations or, at least, long weekends.
- The only way to get any rest is to opt for a simple, elective surgery with a minimum two-week stay and a full ninety-day recovery period.

❦

LESS PAIN AND MORE GAIN

- Write your children a letter every year on their birthday.
- Read to your kids in a box or in a tree or somewhere special.
- Take the time to stop and watch road machines with your boys.
- Make up stories for your children and then tell them to your kids, complete with voices, over and over again.
- After they start school, they need support, not criticism.
- Never watch television if you can play a board game instead.
- Send your kids surprises through the mail.
- Teach your girls how to put up shelves, install locks, and use a power drill.
- Teach your boys how to cook, clean, and sew.
- Invite your kids' friends over and bake cookies and decorate them.
- Read the classics aloud to your teenagers.
- Never allow a television or telephone in their bedrooms.
- Don't buy them a car; make them work for it.
- Never criticize your daughter-in-law; she has your son now.
- And, most importantly, be able to laugh at yourself. Getting naked and looking in the mirror is a sure way to start.

I hope these letters have inspired you to stop right now and write a letter to your children, no matter how old they are. If you don't have children yet, write one to your mother.

If you haven't been as fortunate as I've been to have such a wonderful relationship with your mother, don't be discouraged. As I've said many times in this book, your heavenly Father is interested in being involved in every aspect of your life. He wants to and can reach out to that five-year-old inside you and hug you with words.

A few of my favorite love letters from my heavenly Father are John 17, Psalm 139, and Romans 8:35–39. After you read His letters to you, write one to Him. Telling the Lord how much you love Him and why is what praise and worship are all about, and it's a perfect anecdote for loneliness because the Bible says that the Lord "inhabits the praises of His people" (Psalm 22:3).

Twenty-One

The Family Dream

s I mentioned earlier, Steve, Tucker, Haven, Clancy, and I are traveling across the United States in an RV, discovering that God is alive and well in our nation if only you'll look for Him. I'm writing a book called *Finding God in America,* and all of us are making memories that will last a lifetime. And the best part about it is that we are together 24/7/365! Being an on-the-road mom is even more fun than being a stay-at-home mom. This is what I call "receiving a hundred times over" anything I gave up for Jesus' sake.

Let me tell you how this whole thing got started. When my first book, *Creative Correction,* was released, my publisher asked me if I would be willing to go on a press tour. That book had already cost me way too much time away from my family, and I wasn't about to leave them again. So I answered jokingly, "Only if I can take my family with me." I knew that

that was out of the question—the cost of airfares alone would be astronomical. But after I hung up the phone, my brain kicked into high gear. *What if we didn't have to fly? What if we could drive from city to city?*

That was the beginning of what we now refer to as "The Family Dream." I envisioned the five of us spending a year traversing the nation in an RV, camping in national parks, taking factory tours, and studying historical sites while promoting my book and speaking at churches on the weekends. It would be a press tour/homeschool adventure/family bonding time.

At that point, I should have called it "The Family Fantasy." As you can imagine, there were quite a few obstacles to overcome, hoops to jump through, and pieces to put in place. Number one on the list was how we would pay for a trip like this. And what about Steve's job? Our house? Our dog?

The Lord started by giving us a dream, and then He made it come true. The first thing He did was to provide Steve with a second job, one that he could do away from home. For years, Steve had been volunteering his time to produce our church denomination's conventions. They had gotten so big that the denominational headquarters offered to make his position official, complete with a paycheck. As long as Steve has his computer, phone, fax, and e-mail, he can work from anywhere, even sitting next to the world's largest ball of twine in Minnesota.

The next confirmation for us was the grace and enthusiasm with which our pastors, Steve's bosses, accepted our proposal. They have sent us off with blessings and are looking upon our trip as both a sabbatical for Steve and an extension ministry for the church.

Our house was another big issue. We knew that it would be difficult to find someone willing to lease our house for only a year. And then there was the problem of what to do with our things. Would we need to store them? If not, it was even more critical that we find just the right person to live there and take good care of everything.

God was way ahead of us. It *just so happened* that King's College and Seminary, which is affiliated with our church, was hiring a lady from Kansas City to develop a new department. She would be available to fill the position for only one year, and one of her primary concerns was that she be able to keep her apartment back home. Not only is God good at the big things, like creating the world, but He's also not too shabby when it comes to the little details.

And one of those little things, which was actually a really big deal, was the question of what we were going to do with our dog, Checkers. A seventy-five-pound Dalmatian was way too big to take with us. He was also already ten years old—in other words, in doggie years he was eligible for AARP (I guess that would be AARF to him, wouldn't it?).

I was especially close to Checkers, so I prayed about this quite a bit. Being his "mother," I loved him in spite of his propensity to run inside the house every time the door was left open, jump up on the table, and eat whatever was within paw's reach—especially if it was fresh homemade bread the neighbor had just dropped off.

I was also sympathetic whenever there was a thunderstorm and Checkers, in terror, would jump *through* the screen door; run through the house sopping wet; and land on our good furniture, shaking from head to tail.

Checkers's behavior was legendary among our friends and was the source of many a dig like: "You need to find a book called *Creative Doggie Correction.*" Needless to say, given the unique combination of his mature years and immature ways, I accepted the sad fact that it would be next to impossible to find a friend to keep Checkers for us while we were gone.

I left this dilemma in the Lord's hands with these words, "Father, if You are in this dream of ours, then You have already figured out the perfect solution for our beloved family dog."

I'm glad I stopped trying to understand God a long time ago. He worked it out all right, but certainly not the way I would have handled it. In hindsight I can see that His plan was perfect, but it sure appeared that He had let us down on this one. Shortly after that prayer, Checkers died.

We knew that something was wrong when he no longer jumped up on Clancy and knocked her down whenever she went outside. We took him to the vet, and the X rays revealed lung cancer. I probably took Checkers's death the hardest, but I also had a bizarre peace knowing that God doesn't make mistakes. My kids watch a cartoon video entitled *All Dogs Go to Heaven.* I don't know if that theology stands up, but it helps me to think that Checkers is there, probably sitting sopping wet on my good furniture in my mansion.

The final and most important piece of this puzzle—the

RV itself—was the last piece to fall into place. Why is it that God likes to wait until the last minute to come through? I'm sure it has something to do with testing our faith, but in cases like these, it's more like a pop quiz, and I've always hated those.

For months I searched for the best deal on an RV. I had joined three RV groups, subscribed to two RV magazines, and bought every RV book Amazon.com had to offer. My Internet favorites folder was stuffed with RV links. I was RV ready! I had overlooked only one minor detail—buying the RV.

I thought I had thought of everything. I had it all figured out how we could finance the trip once we got on the road. Nick at Nite had begun airing reruns of *The Facts of Life,* which meant, as I told my husband, that I had really made it as a has-been. On the other hand, I was now considered "retro-cool," and the resurgence of my popularity gave me a platform to reach a whole new generation. I would be able to speak at churches and sell my books to make the RV payment. Steve's salary would cover gas, meals, and RV hookups.

The issue of a down payment on an RV reared its ugly head when I found the perfect motor home for sale on the Internet. It was big, beautiful, and used—a winning combination. I called about it on Superbowl Sunday and made an appointment to see it the next day. It was love at first sight. The gorgeous, forty-five-foot motor coach was ideal for the five of us, and since there were only a couple of glitches that needed to be worked out, we left a deposit check for it and considered ourselves motor home owners.

Beware of those little glitches—they'll get ya every time. I remembered reading something in one of my magazines about it being illegal in the state of California to drive a motor home over forty feet in length. But everyone was doing it, and nobody ever got pulled over. Besides, we were only going to be in California for the first week of our trip.

We must sound just like little kids to God sometimes.

I didn't stop at rationalizing; I proceeded right on to manipulating. I discovered that if we set up a limited liability corporation (LLC) in Montana, we could register the RV to a Montana address, thus skirting the law that wouldn't allow us as California residents to buy a motor home that big. Our proof that this really must be a God thing was the bonus fact that in Montana there is no sales tax.

All we had to do now was come up with the down payment. We made an appointment at our bank and took out a second on our house. That wasn't quite enough, so we also filled out one of those "zero percent down, zero finance charge, you must be a real zero to believe this really won't cost you anything" credit card applications we receive in the mail daily.

Steve and I had sworn off credit cards, but for this we thought we could make an exception. We had it all worked out on paper, and if it all worked out in reality, we would be able to pay everything back in six months.

Our next step was to secure a loan. Interest rates were in our favor, and we received a bottom line quote. We filled out the application and sent it in, along with tax returns from the two previous years. The initial response was very encouraging. The loan company reported that we had excellent credit. (Thank God for the Year of Jubilee, when past mistakes fall off your credit report.) Therefore, we were shocked when they called the next day to tell us that we had been turned down. They recommended that we try another company. We FedExed another set of papers, only to be turned down by that company as well.

They both offered the same explanation. It didn't matter how we planned to make money next year to pay for the trip, they were only interested in the bottom line of our previous tax returns, which clearly revealed that we couldn't afford to purchase an RV on a pastor's and homemaker's salaries.

At this point I started to pay attention to a little inner voice I had been stifling. Just the week before, I had remarked offhandedly to a friend, "The way this whole money thing is going down doesn't fit God's MO. It's hard for me to imagine that He would want us to get into so much debt in order to make this dream happen. But I can't see any other way for it to work."

I told the voice to be quiet and got back to work. I found one more RV loan company and tried again. Two days later we received the good news/bad news. They had approved the loan, but they wouldn't deal with the limited liability corporation in Montana, and they wouldn't finance the sales tax. In essence, this meant that instead of a 20 percent down payment, we would have to come up with 28 percent. We were already hocked to the hilt; there was no way we could come up with more cash.

Friends and family encouraged us to wake up and realize

that The Family Dream was just that—a dream. But it would have taken more faith for me to abandon the dream than to continue to trust God to make it come true.

On an impulse, I picked up the phone and called Tiffin Motorhomes in Red Bay, Alabama. Steve and I had fallen in love with their Allegro Bus at an RV rally we had attended and kept the brochure just to drool over. We knew we couldn't afford a brand-new motor home.

I had heard that the president of the company was a Christian, so when I called that afternoon, I asked if he was in the office. When Mr. Tiffin got on the line, he was as nice as nice could be. I told him about the trip we wanted to take and asked if he would be willing to rent the Allegro Bus to us for the year in exchange for the promotion and publicity we could provide. I told him that I understood that companies wouldn't normally consider this kind of request, but I thought I would ask, just in case. He asked me to fax over a proposal telling him a little more about our goals and plans and said that he would get back to me the next day. So I did.

When I talked with Mr. Tiffin the next day, he said, "Lisa, we really believe in what you and your family want to do. It is just the kind of thing our company would like to be a part of. We would love to see more families be able to spend this kind of time together and make these kinds of memories."

Now, this is the part where God really shines. Mr. Tiffin went on to say, "I've talked this over with my wife and sons, and we think you should use the forty-foot coach as opposed to the thirty-seven-foot coach you requested. And it would be beneficial to both of us if we could make it two coaches instead of one. That way we could trade it out after six months of accumulated miles. Also, if you can wait a couple of months, our 2002 model will be rolling off the line, and it will have a few more amenities."

God does abundantly more than we could ever ask or think! (Ephesians 3:20).

I was beyond excited but tried to contain myself until I got off the phone. After thanking him profusely, I asked, "So that we can budget accordingly, how much will we need to set aside to rent this?"

He answered, "We've decided that we want to loan this to you for the year. Just mention us a couple of times in your book."

That's easy enough—Tiffin Motorhomes, Tiffin Motorhomes, Tiffin Motorhomes, Tiffin Motorhomes, Tiffin Motorhomes!

I learned something huge that day: If God is really in something, we don't have to take shortcuts, tell little white lies, or manipulate the circumstances.

It has always boggled my mind that Abraham would lie rather than trust God to protect him. As told in Genesis 20, the story goes that Abraham and his wife, Sarah, were traveling through a foreign country when out of fear that the king would kill him to get to her, Abraham told Sarah to lie and tell everyone that she was his sister. The truth be told (or the half-truth in this case), they did both have the same father, but she was way more his wife than his sister.

After all He had done, why couldn't Abraham simply trust God to prove that He would take care of him? Why couldn't I trust God to provide an RV for me, legally and without debt, after all He had done to prove that He would take care of me?

Human nature, I guess. We get afraid when we can't see how God is going to make something work out. Or we get worried that He's not going to step in in time. Once we begin to respond out of fear or impatience, we start taking things out of God's hands and putting them into our own.

I hope you will learn from my mistake and realize that God is never late; it just feels that way. Whatever your dream is, He actually has it all worked out ahead of time. Have you gotten anxious and taken shortcuts, told little white lies, or manipulated the circumstances to make your dreams come true? Don't give in by taking things into your own hands; wait for God to work. Why settle for the natural when you can have the supernatural?

Twenty-two

Platform Diving

ome might say it's because my mother always told me
I could be anything I wanted to be; others might
write it off as a sense of destiny. I've also heard it
referred to as a *calling*. Whatever you call it, I've always
known that God had a special plan for my life.

From the moment I gave my life to the Lord, He accepted
it and began using me. Upon returning to school the next
year, I gave the usual "What I Did Last Summer" oral report
to my sixth-grade classmates by giving my testimony and
telling them how they could give their lives to the Lord right
there in homeroom. I started a Bible study in the cafeteria at
lunchtime with my best friend, a pastor's kid named Paul
Linkletter.

Outside of school, I led a little neighbor girl to invite
Jesus into her heart on our backyard swing set. At eleven, I

memorized the parable of the three trees, a story about the life of Christ, and performed it during happy hour at a theater where I was performing in a musical. Before becoming a mouseketeer, I had applied to attend a private school. One of the requirements was to write an essay about your best friend. I wrote mine about Jesus.

First Timothy 4:12 says, "Don't let anyone look down on you because you are young" (NIV). As you can tell, God takes seriously children that take Him seriously, so I want to pause and speak directly to any young person reading this book. You don't have to wait until you are grown to be used by God. He has plans for you now. No one else can touch a child like another child; nobody can get through to a teenager like another teenager. You have a special role that only you, at the age you are now, can fill.

That's how I felt when I moved to California to become a child-actress. I was determined to use whatever platform the Lord gave me to dive straight into telling others about my faith. With every door the Lord opened to me, I discovered a new opportunity to impact people's lives with His love for them.

While I was on *The Facts of Life,* I didn't aspire to become a singer, and I had absolutely no illusions about my singing abilities, but I knew that I wanted to use my celebrity to touch the lives of the young people watching the show. I knew that I could speak to youth groups all day long, but I also realized that if I could put my message to music, it would be much more entertaining and would get to their hearts through the back door. So I recorded an album.

When anything eighties suddenly became hip a few years ago, I granted a wave of "Where Are They Now?" interviews. I saw them as an opportunity to extol the values of motherhood and a chance to portray homeschooling in a positive light.

I've already shared with you that the only reason I'm writing books is because of the potential to reach a significant number of people through the written word. Having recently discovered the power of the Internet to unite people, I am pouring myself into building my Web site community at www.lisawhelchel.com.

I am also in the early stages of beginning a ministry to encourage and provide resources for moms to get together in each other's homes for "MomTime." This would be two hours every week just for them, focusing on food, faith, fellowship, and fun. I have hosted my own group for mothers for ten years, and it has preserved my sanity.

I do all of these things in an effort to take seriously the Scripture that I read again this morning in my devotions: "Much is required from those to whom much is given, and much more is required from those to whom much more is given" (Luke 12:48). I'm sure you'll agree that I qualify for the "much more is given" category. The Lord has abundantly blessed me all of my life. I'm not trying to pay Him back for all of His wonderful gifts; I just realize that He gave them to me to give away. He gave me more than I would ever need when He gave me Himself, and anything above that I want to share with others.

I'm not one of God's favorite children. Ask any mom or

dad—it would be impossible to choose favorites, even for us fallible parents. God has a special plan for each of His children, and it's really not that difficult to find His will for your life. I remember fretting about it as a teenager, wanting so desperately to find it but not even knowing where to begin looking. If I had only relaxed, I would have realized sooner that God's will finds me as long as I walk close to Him.

I seem to stumble on to almost all of the major turning points in my life. If you look back over the stories I've shared with you in this book, I think you'll see what I mean.

It all started because I wanted to go someplace where I could wear a dress. From there I walked down the church aisle, not understanding where I was headed but knowing who was going to meet me there.

I went from being a shy wallflower in Texas to a child-actress in California because my letters arrived just in time for me to get an audition and make the final cut for the mouseketeers.

I was *this* close to accepting a role on a different sitcom that ended up lasting only two seasons. Instead, I enjoyed nine years as Blair, who by the way, would have gotten away with being nice if it hadn't been for a chance turn of phrase during the audition.

Believe it or not, I thank God for the actors' strike. If I hadn't gained all that weight, I might not have established early on one of the cornerstones of my life: spending time with Jesus every day.

It's apparent that God's will found me when I met my husband, but I would have to say that having three children

Parents! When time-outs don't work,
~READ~

Drawing from her own family's experience and her interaction with other parents, Lisa Whelchel offers creative solutions for parents looking for new approaches to discipline. In addition to advice on topics such as sibling conflict and lying, Whelchel offers a biblical perspective and encouragement to parents who are feeling overwhelmed. A handy reference guide with ideas for specific situations rounds out this resource that will be a blessing to parents and their children.

ISBN 1-56179-901-7
Tyndale House Publishers